D0922155

The Nonprofit Management Casebook

Scenes from the Frontlines

Gary M. Grobman

White Hat Communications
Harrisburg, Pennsylvania

The Nonprofit Management Casebook

Scenes from the Frontlines

Published by:
White Hat Communications
Post Office Box 5390
Harrisburg, PA 17110-0390 U.S.A.
717-238-3787 (voice)
717-238-2090 (fax)
http://www.whitehatcommunications.com

All rights reserved. No part of this book may be reproduced or transmitted in any form or by any means, electronic or mechanical, including photocopying, recording or by any information and retrieval system without written permission from the publisher, except for the inclusion of brief quotations in a review.

Copyright © 2010 by Gary M. Grobman

The author can be contacted by e-mail at:
gary.grobman@paonline.com

Note: The cases in this volume are purely works of fiction and any resemblance between the characters and persons living or dead is purely coincidental.

Library of Congress Cataloging-in-Publication Data

Grobman, Gary M.
  The nonprofit management casebook : scenes from the frontlines / Gary M. Grobman.
    p. cm.
  ISBN 978-1-929109-23-4
  1. Nonprofit organizations--Management--Case studies. 2. Nonprofit organiza-
tions--Case studies. I. Title.

HD62.6.G7624 2010
658'.048--dc22

                    2009031167

The Nonprofit Management Casebook
Scenes from the Frontlines

Table of Contents

Introduction

The Nonprofit Management Casebook: Scenes from the Frontlines is the result of a passion I have had for several years to create educational materials that both teach and entertain. My first exposure to this concept was back in the mid-1990s when, as a Ph.D. student, I discovered novels written by Dr. Eliyahu M. Goldratt, a business consultant who created the Theory of Constraints and used fiction to teach the concepts of his management theories about removing bottlenecks in manufacturing processes. What a wonderful medium to use to explain otherwise dry concepts of management!

When I was studying for my master's degree, I took courses that relied exclusively on cases to generate class discussion. I continue to remain impressed by the way cases generate engagement and can illustrate dilemmas that encourage the sharing of diverse points of view by students. Although I continue to believe that a well-written textbook remains valuable, I also feel that well-written cases can play a positive role in educating students.

Finding the right cases, particularly those that may be useful in nonprofit management courses, however, can be elusive. As the author of the introductory nonprofit management textbook, *Introduction to the Nonprofit Sector: A Practical Approach for the 21st Century,* I constantly seek feedback to improve that book, which will soon be in its third edition. Some faculty who use this book suggested that I include a few cases that illustrate some of the lessons on ethics, financial management, human resources, fundraising, and the use of technology.

My intent was to try my hand at writing a few cases and add them to the next edition of the textbook. Because I had so much fun writing, I was unable to stop once I completed the first four, my original objective. Before I knew it, I had enough for a stand-alone casebook.

My inspiration for these stories came from a variety of sources. For more than 13 years, I was the CEO of a small nonprofit state association, and I encountered many management dilemmas during that time. I have also spent an additional 13 years writing about nonprofit organizations and providing consulting services to national, state, and local nonprofits. Every situation in these cases came out of my imagination. The cases have been designed to illustrate important lessons that I try to share in my general nonprofit textbooks, but in a more entertaining format. I made an effort to provide a variety of nonprofit settings, such as associations, long-term care facilities, universities, human service agencies, advocacy organizations, and think tanks, among others.

All of these cases are fictional, and any similarity between the organizations and characters in these cases and actual organizations and individuals is purely coincidental. But I would suggest that the situations that occur in these cases are not farfetched. They *could* be actual situations one might encounter when managing or governing a nonprofit organization.

I've begun this collection of cases with *Jane's Dilemma: Hiring the Development Director.* In this case, the executive director of a foundation faces several ethical dilemmas simultaneously. She and her organization have paid a heavy price for her abrogation of her responsibilities to supervise the investments made on behalf of the organization by a trusted employee. And she is being held accountable for that failure. When given an opportunity to recover from this traumatic experience, she must choose between doing what is right (and potentially pay a heavy personal cost for doing so) or taking advantage of an ethically distasteful solution to all of her problems. Even if she does choose the "right" response, there are issues involved with respect to communications among herself, her board chair, and her board about the situation in which she finds herself.

I Choose to Live Foundation—One Man's Vision to Form a New Charity is the story of a new startup. According to the IRS, even at a time when economic output has been shrinking, the number of nonprofit organizations applying for charitable tax exempt status was 79,236 in 2008, and many more than that number were incorporated that year in the 50 states. The theme of this story is not atypical of many I come across in my consulting work with those who wish to give birth to a new organization. An individual has a vision of addressing a particular social problem of interest by creating an instrument that will harness the power of others. Yet that individual often will feel constrained by the appropriate separation between managing and governing, or other limitations that apply to organizations that receive substantial public benefits in exchange for following certain laws and regulations. The recognition that it is appropriate to form a public board consisting of members who are not either relatives or personal friends of the entrepreneur starting the organization appears to me to be more of an exception than the rule.

Cutting the Budget of the Harristown Family Service addresses an important issue for every nonprofit organization—finding enough resources during times of retrenchment. During economically challenging times, demand for the services provided by nonprofit organizations often expands at the same time that revenue from all sources shrinks. Most nonprofit organizations rarely have surplus resources even in the best of economic times. When a recession hits, nonprofit organizations are disproportionately affected. In this case, the executive director utilizes a particular change management tool, Large Group Intervention, to engage her staff in discussing possible strategies to close a serious budget shortfall. For more information about this tool and others, see Chapter 15 of my textbook, *Introduction to the Nonprofit Sector*.

HHA's Dilemma: Be a Good Citizen or Fight Extortion presents a public policy issue that is increasingly of importance to those nonprofits that own property in distressed communities. More and more, local governments see nonprofit organizations, particularly hospitals, nursing homes, and universities, as sources of potential revenue. The pressure on nonprofit organizations to make payments to local governments for services during times of economic distress increases when tax increases are not politically feasible. And, as I make a case in Chapter 27 of my book for practitioners, *The Nonprofit Handbook (5th Edition)*, a case can be made that those nonprofits that can make some contribution to local governments for the services they receive should be open to doing so—at least on a voluntary basis. But there is nothing "voluntary" about having a choice of negotiating a payment-in-lieu-of-taxes agreement with a local government or having to invest tens of thousands of dollars and hundreds of staff hours in a court fight to protect an organization's tax exemption. Some organizations might take a pragmatic view of this choice and pursue the path that would result in the least revenue loss over the long term. Others might take a different approach, choosing to resist, particularly when they perceive that the law is on their side. For more than a decade, I was intimately involved in addressing this issue in Pennsylvania as an advocate for scores of nonprofit hospitals, nursing homes, schools, umbrella fundraising organizations, family services, and others facing the very choice that the CEO of the long-term care facility in this case faces. It is with some pride that I can point to a law passed by the Pennsylvania General Assembly that was quite favorable to the position of charities on this issue, and the success of several judicial interventions, in the form of amicus briefs filed with the Pennsylvania Supreme Court, that assisted in favorable rulings. For more specific information on the general issue of nonprofit tax exemptions, see chapter 27 of *The Nonprofit Handbook*.

   When I first started writing *Museum and Historical Association State Budget Cuts*, in the winter of 2009, state governments were just beginning to recognize that massive revenue shortfalls were on the horizon. Totally by coincidence, alternative budgets were introduced in Pennsylvania a few months later that actually did zero out programs supporting museums in the state, and it was a possibility that a final budget agreement would codify such a policy. Closing a $3 billion budget shortfall within a $29 billion budget presents a major challenge in a state such as Pennsylvania. And considering that hardly anyone in the state legislature is willing to consider a general tax increase and federal entitlement programs are legally required to provide increased funding, there is not much room for funding programs that don't directly affect public health and safety. Many individuals strongly feel, as I do, that programs affecting the arts and humanities are essential to the quality of life we all treasure, and merit protection. In this particular case, the executive director of this association must find a way to protect the interests of her members and advocate for funding at a time when finding dollars for this purpose will be difficult.

Blackberries, blogs, Facebook, Twitter, iPhones—one can come up with a list of dozens of new technologies that have changed the face of organizational communication. Our children have grown up with these and take them for granted. But some of us continue to resist, despite many advantages they offer. The tools one uses to run a modern nonprofit have changed, and those who haven't mastered them are in danger of seriously constraining organizational effectiveness. *Evaluating Dr. Luddite, Harristown Asperger's Syndrome Foundation Executive Director* involves the case of an otherwise exemplary nonprofit CEO who has failed to adjust to the demands of communication techniques in the 21st century. This case also illustrates another aspect of nonprofit organization boards—not everyone on the board shares the same view with respect to the organization's mission. This contrasts to a board of a for-profit organization, which, in theory, is to make as much money as possible for the organization's stockholders. It is not unusual for nonprofit organization boards to have members, or groups of members, with their own agendas. It is also not unusual for a board meeting to get "out of hand" and require substantial interpersonal skills by the board chair, and a deft use of *Robert's Rules of Order* when necessary, to keep things under control. A few years ago, a new issue surfaced of interest to the nonprofit sector—how prepared organizations in the sector are with respect to leadership succession. Beyond the immediate issue of dealing with a long-term CEO who refuses to harness the new technologies to the foundation's advantage, the board must begin to think of how it would deal with finding that CEO's replacement, should he be removed or in the event he retires.

Case 7, *Navigating a Dual Relationship at the Public Interest Policy Center*, involves a delicate situation that highlights issues relating to an inappropriate power relationship between a funder and an organization. In this case, the relationship is clearly inappropriate, unethical, and bordering on the illegal. Perhaps belatedly, the CEO has reported this to her board, and the board faces sensitive political issues in a quest to resolve the problem. It is not unusual, however, for a funder to place substantial burdens on organizations to which it makes grants. In any case, people are, well, *human*. It is not unusual for harmful personal relationships to develop between staff members of an organization, board members and staff members, board members and other board members, and staff and other organization stakeholders. Complicated ethics issues often ensue in which decisions are made when there is not an arms-length relationship between the parties, and decisions may not be made that are totally in the interest of the organization.

To the central character of *Gambling on an Outside Fundraising Consultant for the "For the Kids" Shelter*, getting the required approval of her board for a new program is perceived to be a slam dunk. This case highlights issues relating to the sharing of decision-making power between board and staff. In this case, the organization's CEO has not performed due diligence with respect to checking out a prospective partner, and has failed to consider many important issues that she should have before presenting a proposal to the board. CEOs of nonprofit organizations are constantly bombarded with proposals from for-profit organizations to engage in collaborations. Many of these proposals are certainly win-win situations and make sense to pursue. In this case, there are certainly clear red flags that should give the CEO pause about participating in this particular program.

There are many issues that arise when individuals observe misconduct within their organizations. Should they report it? If so, to whom? What protection might they have from retaliation for reporting misconduct? *Reporting Financial Misconduct at Uncommon Agenda* considers these issues, and adds another complication, as the observer of the misconduct is a personal friend of the perpetrator. The protagonist of this story outlines eight possible actions he might take to respond to his serendipitously obtained knowledge about serious misconduct by a personal friend and colleague at the nonprofit advocacy organization where they both work, each of which has costs and benefits. There is a myth that federal whistleblower protection laws protect whistleblowers in nonprofit organizations from retaliation. As this case makes clear, federal law provides only limited protection for whistleblowers in such organizations. Nonprofit organizations should have written policies that encourage their employees to report misconduct internally without fearing retaliation for doing so.

Case 10, *The Disruptive Board Member of the Harristown Vet Center* is the story of a board member with some obvious mental health issues. He is creating unwelcome distractions at board meetings and at the headquarters of the organization. Someone has to do something, but there are complications and adverse consequences to simply removing him from the board. More often, board members need to be removed simply because they are unproductive. It is an important task of the chair of the board to keep all board members informed, engaged, and participating. As this case provides evidence, it requires sensitivity and substantial leadership skills for a board chair to be successful.

When does loyalty to one's nonprofit organization take precedence over one's responsibility to be loyal to his or her profession? *Public Relations Dilemma at the Harristown Hospital and Health System* examines a situation in which an honest and ethical public relations professional faces a dilemma concerning how to "spin" a particular ethics situation that has somehow leaked to the media. This particular staff member has voiced his concern about the consequences of one particular decision, but has been unsuccessful in convincing his colleagues to take the "high road." Now, he may be in the unenviable position of being called upon to "publicly" defend that decision, which understandably makes him very uncomfortable.

As both a nonprofit organization CEO and a for-profit provider of services to nonprofit organizations, I have been on both sides of the table with respect to forging agreements between nonprofits and for-profits. It has been clear to me that there is a distinct difference in the time it takes each of these parties to make decisions. In *Approving a Partnership Agreement—Board Paralysis at the State Association*, I illustrate some of the obstructions that have served as a barrier to one state association approving a partnering agreement with a for-profit vendor in a timely manner. Although the facts of this hypothetical case may appear to be quite extreme, I know of real cases that were even more egregious than this one. Delays in obtaining final board approval for an agreement are perhaps inevitable and emanate from many factors, including the diffusion of power within a board, board diversity, and a less than homogeneous perspective on the mission of the organization compared to for-profits. I think that nonprofit boards also provide less authority for staff to make decisions than do their for-profit counterparts.

In *The State Volunteer Firefighters Association's Dilemma,* a respected, long-time association CEO is suspected of writing a tell-all book that is perceived as embarrassing to both his organization and his profession. During a hastily-called telephone conference call, board members discuss how to respond. Should he be summarily fired? Should the organization claim book royalties as its own because much of the information came from protected organizational sources? What has this professional done that is "wrong"? This case serves to point out that organizations should have clear written policies outlining what is expected of their staff members, including what outside income may be permitted or proscribed, and what organizational documents and other internal communications are considered proprietary.

There are certainly many benefits of one person in an organization doing the bulk of the work. And there are costs, as well. *The One (Wo)Man Band Running the Kenmore Midget Baseball League* illustrates that organizations may pay a high price for permitting one person to have too much power over organizational decision-making. In this particular case, that one person is generally selfless and honest and wants to do whatever is in the best interests of the kids in her program. Yet as this case makes clear, she does not have any understanding about certain ethical concepts that must be understood by those who manage and govern nonprofit organizations, such as conflicts of interest and dual relationships. All board members of a nonprofit must be active players in organizational governing, and this board, as a whole, has abrogated its responsibility to both govern the organization and assure that it is managed properly.

Nonprofit institutions of higher education are unlike any other nonprofit organizations, in many respects. I have served as both an employee and as a private contractor to such institutions as an adjunct professor for more than five years. During that time, I have been an observer of their organizational cultures. Each, while unique, shares some aspects that I find fascinating. In *The Professor's Farewell*, a tenured professor is sharing his frustrations with being pushed out after four decades with a particular university. I use this case to illustrate some unusual facets about this particular nonprofit setting. While some of what appears in this case is intended to be tongue-in-cheek, reviewers of this case who have been full-time college professors for decades have told me that most of what appears here is quite plausible, from their experience. In any event, issues such as tax-exempt property, the extent to which the market sets pricing, and the "politics" of working for a large nonprofit organization are among those that are featured. I've generally had good experiences working for educational institutions, but I have occasionally seen management practices that simply leave my head shaking in disbelief.

How would you respond as a CEO if you discovered that one of your most trusted and productive employees exaggerated his credentials in order to obtain his job? In this particular case, *Doctoring the Résumé—Giving the Third Degree to the Director of Research at SCRC,* there are several viable options for the CEO to consider, none of which is particularly attractive. This case also considers the pros and cons of creating a culture that encourages personal friendships among staff within an organization.

Acknowledgments

Many individuals played a role in bringing this volume to fruition. I would like to first thank my wife, a professional editor and publisher, for her support during my writing of this book, and for her editing skills. Without her contributions, this book would never have been written.

I benefitted from the feedback provided by a cadre of volunteer reviewers of these cases, recruited from my colleagues from ARNOVA, the Association for Research on Nonprofit Organizations and Voluntary Action. Among those who made contributions that improved these cases were Dr. Salvatore Alaimo of Grand Valley State University; Dr. Paul Grovikar of Northern Ohio University; Dr. Peter Dobkin Hall of the Hauser Center for Nonprofit Organizations at Harvard University and the City University of New York (CUNY); Dr. Leigh Hersey of the University of Memphis; Margery Saunders of SUNY Brockport; Alonzo Villarreal, Jr. of Transformation Strategies; and Dr. Kerri Mollard of Ohio Dominican University.

Thanks also go to ARNOVA members Dr. Roger Lohmann, Dr. John McNutt, and Dr. Felice Perlmutter, who answered some of my questions about various aspects of the culture of institutions of higher learning—the setting of one particular case—and Dale Laninga, who provided insight into long-term care facilities.

Linda Grobman and John Hope made substantial contributions to this effort with their editing and proofreading skills, and both offered many suggestions that I incorporated into this casebook.

And, of course, I am most grateful to my nonprofit clients; readers of my textbooks and books for practitioners; and my students at Indiana University of Pennsylvania, Gratz College, and Marylhurst University for inspiring many of the stories that comprise these cases.

Gary M. Grobman
August 2009

Case 1

Jane's Dilemma—Hiring the Development Director

"Thank you, and I appreciated our meeting," Jane said, rising to shake Bernie Plotkoff's hand. She would have preferred to avoid this customary gesture at the end of such a meeting, but she knew it would have been rude to do so. "I'll be in touch soon, perhaps next week, about whether you were the successful candidate for this position," she added stiffly, trying to conjure up a smile—which was a struggle, considering the circumstances.

Jane's stomach knotted up, and she began to sweat profusely as she considered her options, none of which were attractive.

For fifteen years, Jane Doesky had devoted herself to making the A. K. Schwarzkin Charitable Foundation the best charity it could be. She was well-paid as the executive director of the organization, and the income was now much more necessary than when she was first hired, because her mother was in a nursing home, and she was making payments of $6,000 each month to the home. Mom showed increasing signs of developing Alzheimer's, and Jane feared that this would necessitate having her moved to a unit that provided services to these patients, with a substantially higher monthly charge.

Jane had sacrificed her personal life, making herself available to the organization 24/7. She had the usual number of crises during her tenure, but had always come through with solutions that were creative. Her colleagues in the general nonprofit community held her in high esteem for her integrity and leadership.

Now, it appeared that not only was her job on the line, but the continued existence of the charity was at risk. It was a perfect storm that had put her in this unenviable situation—a flagging economy, the trust of a friend and colleague that was violated, and the resignation of the organization's dependable, long-time Director of Development and de facto chief financial officer, Myron Cohn, for "personal reasons." Almost everyone knew what those "personal reasons" were by now, as the newspapers had had a field day documenting the financial scandal that had rocked the Jewish charitable community in general and the Schwarzkin charity in particular.

Cohn had fallen hook, line, and sinker for the Madoff Ponzi scheme, investing most of the foundation's assets, lured by a promise of returns that were substantially better than the market. Doesky had trusted Cohn's judgment, providing only cursory oversight over his financial management, recognizing that he had an exemplary track record and almost 20 years more experience than she had. Once it became evident that $30 million in Foundation assets were gone with virtually no chance of any recovery, Myron had submitted his resignation, content to retire to a comfy condo in Florida. Leaving Jane and the Foundation holding the bag. An empty bag.

Jane thought back to her meeting a month before with her board chair, Goldie Sharafsky, who had been livid after hearing about how much the Foundation had lost. She had summoned Jane to her own office, located in a posh, downtown office building adjacent to Rittenhouse Square in Philadelphia. Once there, she had provided Jane with a deftly-delivered ultimatum.

"I'll be frank," Goldie had begun, closing the door for privacy, her tone of voice masking any cordiality that had usually been there whenever Jane was asked, infrequently, to meet in Goldie's office. More often, meetings between the two were held over a casual lunch in one of the trendy cafés along Broad Street. Jane did not expect this meeting to be pleasant, but she felt blindsided by what followed.

"I've exchanged some telephone calls with the Foundation leadership, and we have come to a consensus on how to handle this unpleasant situation with the financial scandal," Goldie began, her words measured. Jane did not take this as a good sign for what was to come.

"Your job is on the line here. Since the Foundation has taken such an unexpected hit from both the scandal and poor fundraising brought on by the tanking of the economy, everyone's job is on the line, including mine as chair. One of our board members, I won't tell you which *mumser* that was but you could probably guess, even suggested liquidating the Foundation. Others wanted to simply fire you and rebuild. Even your supporters are *kvetching.*"

Jane felt the blood rush to her head. But she said nothing. Maintain some control, she thought.

"I fought to keep you. I can't find any justification for simply giving up," Goldie continued. "So many people depend on our programs. And you have considerable talent that I think can work to our advantage as we try to recover from this debacle. I know Myron let you down, and God knows, I can understand why you let him have free rein over investment policy. But when push comes to shove, you are responsible and accountable for the results of all of the Foundation's employees."

Jane took a deep breath, waiting for the shoe to drop. It did.

"So, here's what we decided. You have two years to rebuild the Foundation's assets to a level that we feel comfortable funding our commitments, and you will be evaluated in a year and must demonstrate that you are making significant progress toward achieving that goal. If you can agree to do that, you can stay; otherwise, we will provide you with two months of severance pay, shake hands, thank you for your service over the years, and launch a search for your successor."

Jane, speechless, shaken, simply nodded her head and left after exchanging the bare minimum of parting pleasantries.

Now back in her office, contemplating what was told to her in confidence by the third candidate she had interviewed that day for the vacant Director of Development position, her anxiety heightened as she considered what he had offered to her.

Bernie Plotkoff was a name well known to her. She was intrigued that he had applied for the vacant position although she granted him an interview more out of curiosity than any realistic expectation that she would actually hire him. He was the current Director of Development for the S.D. Leibman

Foundation, the Swartzkin Foundation's principal competitor for charitable donations directed to serving Jewish adolescent runaways and missing children. Both foundations had been established at about the same time, inspired by the disappearance of Chandra Levy in Washington, D.C. during the summer of 2001. At one time, the boards of both foundations had considered merging, but relations between the two organizations had soured during negotiations and both had gone their separate ways. The board chairs of both organizations at that time had once been personal friends, bonded by the shared trauma of separate, but similar, family tragedies involving young family members.

Yet following the breakup of the proposed merger, they were no longer on speaking terms. While this breakup appeared to be irreconcilable at the time, most board members and staff leadership, including Jane, judged that an eventual merger would be inevitable, particularly when economic times necessitated an end to competition for funds and programs that served essentially the same clients.

Jane had to admit that the Leibman Foundation was the more successful of the two, attributed for the most part to the aggressive fundraising tactics of the development director whom she had just finished interviewing as part of her process to find a successor to Cohn. "Aggressive" was perhaps too polite a word to describe Bernie's fundraising reputation. The Leibman Foundation raised millions of dollars, including from some folks who contributed to both foundations.

The Leibman Foundation's fundraising tactics were anything but low-key. It was among the first to enclose a check in its direct mailings that recipients could cash regardless of whether they made a contribution, instilling an additional level of guilt to make one. It was one of the few Jewish charities that enclosed a small prayer book or religious article such as a yamulke (a skull cap), which would make recipients who were religiously observant to be violative of Jewish law if they simply tossed the mail piece into the trash rather than having it undergo a ritual burial.

It was rumored that Leibman's annual development budget included a line-item for the hiring of a private detective, and that Plotkoff utilized the services of shady Internet database businesses that sold information to anyone for a fee—

information that most of us would assume would not be available publicly to anyone. This was part of what is called "prospect research," what otherwise was a legitimate technique of fundraisers to learn about the capacity of donors and potential donors. As "refined" by Plotkoff, it was more akin to "spying."

In short, the Leibman Foundation sanctioned whatever worked, kept constant pressure on giving, and held over-the-top lavish fundraisers that attracted giving that only minimally was provided because of the organization's mission. And the grand conductor of the fundraising strategy was Bernie Plotkoff, looked upon with undisguised disdain by many of his colleagues, most of whom were secretly envious of the results he recorded for his employer.

Prior to the interview, Jane had no evidence to think that he did anything overtly illegal, although it would not have come as a surprise to her if he routinely crossed the line of ethical conduct without a second thought. If he did so, she would have attributed it to being a zealot for the cause, and she wouldn't have expected that he violated professional ethics for his own personal gain. Now that she had finished her interview with him and heard his pitch, she had second thoughts about her judgment about both his ethics and his allegiance to following the letter of the law in pursuing his craft.

What Bernie had offered her was communicated quite directly, and he didn't make any effort to veil his proposal in euphemistic references to make it appear less distasteful to her. She was shocked by his brazen *chutzpah,* and she felt even a bit insulted that he would trust her to keep his offer in confidence.

He offered to leave the Leibman Foundation for Cohn's position, giving two week's notice. He would want his current salary that he received from Leibman, plus a 10% raise. He would want an unvouchered expense account of $20,000 annually and a company car. On top of that, he would expect an annual incentive bonus of 2% of the amount he raised. He would guarantee that he could increase the Foundation's fundraising income by 100% in the first year, and make up most of the losses from the Madoff financial scandal by focusing particularly on donors who had the capacity to participate in planned giving.

What gave Jane even more pause was what he told her would be his strategy for achieving these lofty goals, and when he disclosed that, Jane didn't doubt his ability to come through and save her own job as well as keep the foundation viable for many years to come.

Bernie intimated that he had on disk all of the fundraising records of the Leibman Foundation, including all of the prospect research files and history of giving for 10,000 donors, about four times the number of donors that were in the Schwarzkin fundraising database. Hire him, and he would integrate that disk into the fundraising operations of the Schwarzkin Foundation. Even without this database, his contacts alone would result in millions of dollars in additional donations to the Foundation. And with this database and the files that came with it, the Schwarzkin Foundation's future would be cemented, and its major competitor for donations, the Leibman Foundation, would be crippled. Within a year or two, the Leibman Foundation leadership would be begging for a merger, so the integration of the database files and the end to destructive competition between the two organizations would come to an end. So, while his plan might be somewhat on the shady side, all of the money raised would be going to a cause both organizations support, so in the long run, what would be the harm?

As Jane contemplated how difficult it might be to find another job in this economic environment, she considered the pros and cons of Bernie's proposal.

Discussion Questions:

1. What are Jane's options, and what are the pros and cons of each option?

2. Should Jane report the offer she received from Bernie to anyone within or outside of her organization?

3. How much should the fact that Jane needs to maintain her income to support her mother's nursing home costs factor into her decision? Discuss any conflict between Jane's ethical responsibility to act in the best

interests of the organization and the need to serve her own interests, and how such a conflict should be resolved.

4. How much does the fact that these two organizations are likely to merge sometime in the near future factor into her decision?

5. Discuss the ethics of each of the fundraising strategies used by Bernie Plotkoff.

6. Discuss what is appropriate with respect to prospect research and what are some of the prospect research techniques that might cross the line of acceptability, even if they are effective.

7. Discuss the pros and cons of paying fundraisers based on the amount they raise. Why do almost all organizations that represent fundraisers have ethics codes that consider compensation based on the amount a fundraiser raises to be unethical?

Case 2

I Choose to Live Foundation—One Man's Vision to Form a New Charity

John Buck was a man with a mission and a vision, and he wasn't going to let anyone stand in his way until he got what he wanted. Whatever it was. Whether it was finding a wealthy, socially connected spouse; getting his MBA from Columbia; helping his wife raise twin boys; furnishing a small yet tasteful summer home in the Hamptons; or winning his age group in the New York Marathon (actually, the best he could achieve was third, but he resolved to train hard enough to move up in the national Master's road race rankings each year).

Regardless of the goal of the moment, he focused on it with the concentration of a Zen Master and did whatever it took to achieve his objective—often taking no prisoners. At 60, he felt he was in the prime of his life, and he often referred to his wife of 35 years, Stacy, an attorney who specialized in family law, as his "trophy wife," although she was his first and only love.

He conceded to himself that he often ruffled some feathers, but he had minimal patience for those who found objections, usually specious, for his aggressive problem-solving. Whatever he got involved in, he did so in a manner that did not leave very much out of his control, either at work or managing his personal life.

When he was diagnosed with prostate cancer two years earlier, he initially assumed that he was beginning a downward spiral that would end in a slow, painful death. He was taken totally by surprise by the diagnosis. He had had a routine PSA blood test at the age of 55 to diagnose the presence of an antigen that often shows up in those with this cancer. It had been negative, but even with a positive test, many doctors recommended against aggressive responses because prostate cancer tumors are often so slow developing that most men with this cancer will die from other causes. Regardless, he had learned that prostate cancer was the most common form of cancer among men in the U.S. and the second leading cause of cancer death among men, with only lung cancer having a higher rate.

It was not a positive blood test but rather some difficulty urinating that had triggered the diagnosis, which was confirmed after a biopsy.

Upon hearing the diagnosis, John didn't spend a minute wallowing in self-pity. Rather, beating the disease became another challenge, even when his long-time primary physician had suggested that he might consider simply letting the disease take its course. In consultation with an oncologist he knew from his running club, John had some radiation treatments, took hormones, and eventually underwent surgery to remove his prostate. After a six-month absence, he resumed his running workouts.

Inspiring him to not only survive but to thrive was Lance Armstrong, who at the age of 25 overcame testicular cancer that had spread to his lungs and brain and a prognosis of having only a 50% chance of survival to become one of the greatest athletes in modern history. Almost every day, before his workouts, John would visit the Lance Armstrong Foundation Web site at *http://www.livestrong.org* and create a virtual bond with this icon of the bicycling world who also competed alongside him, somewhere in the crowd, in the New York Marathon.

John networked with other upper middle-class male prostate cancer survivors in Northern New Jersey where he lived and in the Big Apple, where he still worked a modified schedule. Many men he spoke with had survived much longer without the return of cancer, some for as many as ten years. Unlike John, some had gone through the five stages of grief after learning of their diagnosis. Many had suffered bouts of depression. Some had retreated from their friends and families, losing their zest for life. For those with advanced forms of the disease and who were in chronic pain, morphine was one drug of choice. Some turned to an overdependence on other drugs, both prescribed and those that were not, to relieve their physical and psychic pain.

Occasionally, someone in his network died. John's mother had died of breast cancer when she was 60. John remembered that Mom had spiraled into depression, shutting herself off from family and friends, isolating herself in her Manhattan apartment with only a mangy cat for companionship, never venturing out to enjoy what life could offer one even in the clutches of the late stage breast cancer that claimed her life prematurely. The cancer had metastasized to her bones, lungs, and liver. She became emaciated, and her spirit had been ravaged along with her body. John had watched his mother die slowly, receiving daily reports from the nurse whom he had hired to care for her while John managed his hedge funds, earning more in a week than his Mom earned in nearly a lifetime—at least until the Madoff scandal and the economic meltdown of 2008-2009 had encouraged his clients to seek more secure, stable investment options, if they had any assets left to invest.

These men with prostate cancer with whom he networked became his friends and extended family. They would meet in the City to attend Knicks games at Madison Square Garden and have dinner afterwards at trendy, expensive restaurants on the West Side. And they would talk. What they had in common was a resolve not to let cancer claim their spirit and zest for life.

John recognized the therapeutic value of being with others who shared the unique experience of being diagnosed with this killer disease. And he also saw that the stress of this disease accrued not just on the men struck by cancer but on their families.

One of his friends suggested organizing a trip to see the Broadway musical "In the Heights" for nearly a dozen men with advanced stages of prostate cancer in and around John's bedroom community of Harristown, New Jersey, a short 25-minute train ride to Grand Central Station. This might possibly be the last opportunity for independence for some of them before the disease claimed their lives. Most of these men were like John—professional men who would not give a second thought to buying a new suit for $800 if it was both fashionable and functional. But John knew that other men on the invitation list would be making a major financial sacrifice to accept the invitation, and some men were unable to afford the trip at all. Many had lost their livelihoods as a result of their cancer diagnosis, and others were victimized by the economic recession the entire country was sinking into beginning in 2008.

John didn't hesitate in writing a generous check to subsidize the trip for several men whom he knew would not be able to afford to accept this invitation. But this spontaneous philanthropy planted a seed of an idea. Why not start an organization that would be the conduit of charitable contributions for this purpose? At least this way, the funds he was providing out of his own pocket would be tax deductible. And there were hundreds of men who might benefit from programs that would focus on letting those with prostate cancer have some fun and enjoy the precious little time they had left, when most money directed to the issue of prostate cancer seemed to be focused on finding a cure. And unlike the days when his own mother was diagnosed, new drugs and treatments afforded thousands of men and women diagnosed with cancer much better odds for survival, and for longer periods.

John latched on to his idea as if it were a new toy. His wife was smart enough not to discourage him, not that there was anything she could have said that would have convinced him to drop the idea. First, he would begin raising money so he could quit his job as a hedge fund manager (the firm was going under anyway, and employees were talking among themselves about how to negotiate severance packages) and be the full-time director of this new program. Second, he would need to form a board of directors for him to lead. It would have to be a small board, and not have anyone who would interfere with his vision. His wife would be a good choice for Vice-President, he thought, as she was an attorney, and that would come in handy for handling all of the legal affairs of this new organization. Their twin boys, now grown, and one daughter-in-law would also provide some valuable skills and be excellent board members. (He and his wife were not on speaking terms with the other daughter-in-law, after his wife got into an irreconcilable disagreement with her over the color of bridesmaid dresses.)

And perhaps a couple of the men from the network would make good board members, provided they didn't try to run things and would be satisfied with being major donors and finding others to donate. But if they did expect to have more than a cosmetic role, he would be assured of control of at least a majority of votes through his relatives, if anything ever came down to a vote or his influence to direct the activities and substantive programs of the organization was challenged. If that occurred, he would be assured of having enough power to throw anyone off the board who didn't cooperate with his vision.

It has been pointed out by many that board members should be recruited who offer at a minimum, one of the three "W's": wealth, wisdom, or work. In John's mind, the first was a priority, and any of the second or third attributes any of these individuals could bring with them would be gravy.

The ideas for making this dream become a reality were flowing, and he needed to get them down while they were still fresh in his mind.

He took out a pen, found a legal tablet, and started writing down what he would need to do to form his new organization, which he decided to name the "I Choose to Live Foundation."

- Incorporate: New Jersey or NY?
- Recruit board members
- Write bylaws. Gotta keep everything under my control.
- Design a Web site. Reserve a domain name. Should have an area for men to leave their stories about their experiences with diagnosis and treatment and help others with questions. Needs an "Ask the Doctor" page.
- Prepare a fundraising plan. Need to register with anyone to do this? Can raise money at a dinner with a celebrity speaker. Can auction off sports memorabilia online?
- Open a bank account
- Apply for 501(c)(3) tax-exempt status. Does this cost any money??? Can Stacey do this?
- Make sure no one else is using this name. How do I do this?
- Find a celebrity (New York Rangers player?) to be an endorser/sponsor. Maybe a goalie who can help make a "stop" or a goal scorer can help score a goal of helping those with prostate cancer.

Discussion Questions:

1. If John came to you for advice on whether to start this organization, what would you tell him?

2. What would you advise John with respect to the governance model of his organization?

3. What problems might you see if he decides to apply on behalf of this organization for 501(c)(3) tax-exempt status with his current vision of organizational governance?

4. Would you expect this organization to still be around after 20 years?

5. If he did decide not to invest his time in starting a new organization focusing on providing entertainment options for men with prostate cancer, what other options might he have for achieving his goal of providing these services?

6. Should John's organization consider providing its services to those with other forms of cancer?

7. What other tasks should be on John's list of things to do when forming his organization?

Case 3

Cutting the Budget of the Harristown Family Service

The image that kept returning to Sarah Jordan's brain was the scene from *The Wizard of Oz* where water is poured over the wicked witch, who is screaming, "I'm melting, I'm melting!" In this case, the metaphor did not describe Sarah herself but rather the income stream of the Harristown Family Service. At the same time, demand for the organization's services was skyrocketing, fueled by the credit crunch, burgeoning unemployment, and increases in reported child abuse. For the first time in the HFS's history, clients were being turned away for some services, or placed on expanding waiting lists for others.

HFS was 60 years old now, a pillar of the community's social service safety net. Sarah had been at the helm of HFS for 20 years, after serving ten years with the organization as head of the social work department. Although an administrator, she still managed a small social work caseload so she could keep current with the "street level" aspects of her operation. Another reason for this was that she was a "not afraid to roll up your sleeves and get your hands dirty" social worker at heart, continuing to find immense personal satisfaction in working directly with needy clients rather than moving paper around and attending meetings, the two tasks that dominated her daily agenda.

During her tenure, HFS had grown from 10 to 60 employees. Income financing the $5 million annual operating budget came from a balanced mix of fee-for-service payments from clients, private donations, endowment interest, and government and foundation grants. There had been some lean years in the past, but never had the agency experienced a perfect storm of a deteriorating economy that squeezed income and that increased demand for its services from otherwise eligible clients who were unable to afford to pay HFS enough for the agency to recover its costs. These two trends squeezing the organization were exacerbated by simple bad luck and a culture of corporate greed in the general economy.

Now the chickens had come home to roost. Government bailouts had helped the greedy, not the needy, she mused. The banks, insurers, auto manufacturers, and others who had made bad decisions for years were on the short list for help. No one proposed helping the helpers who had played by the rules.

This morning, Sarah had convened a staff meeting with everyone present, from the COO and CFO to the 87-year-old "retired" social worker who answered the telephones. Everyone was there, including Sean Smithson, one of the front-line social workers she would have been quite happy to have come up with some excuse to miss this particular meeting. Sean was the organization's *énfant terrible,* and he could be counted on to provide unwelcome, nonproductive capriciousness in any serious discussion. For years, Sean broke almost every personnel rule, was contemptuous of authority, thumbed his nose at laws and regulations whenever they got in his way, played practical jokes on co-workers that often were over the line, and was a general pain in the butt.

His actions resulted in several near lawsuits filed by clients. Yet, she had to concede, he was the best social worker she had ever had, his risk-taking always in the interest of the organization's clients, even when not particularly good for the organization.

If the TV show *House, M.D.* ever had a spinoff that focused on a social worker rather than a medical doctor, Sean could be the model for the main character. One thing Sarah could count on was that Sean would play class clown and do everything he could to sabotage the tone she intended to set for this brainstorming session. For today's meeting, her tolerance level for levity was as low as it could get, as decisions made to increase income and cut expenses, influenced by input from staff, would determine whether the agency would survive the economic tsunami that threatened to swallow up similar agencies in other communities.

Her memo requiring all staff to attend and participate in this meeting spelled out its purpose—to engage everyone in a group brainstorming session to get input from staff to increase income and cut expenses before she submitted her recommendations to the board at the next meeting in three weeks. The inspiration for including everyone on staff was an experience she had had in graduate school learning about the benefits of large group interventions (LGI).

It was early March, and a light snow was falling. *Perhaps this is the time to announce my retirement,* she thought, imagining herself lounging on a sun-drenched beach in front of a Florida condo with her husband, Harold, and a grandchild or two, worrying about nothing more important than where and when to have lunch later. But then she dismissed this option, recognizing that her leadership was needed to save the organization, not only to protect the livelihoods of the almost three score people in front of her, most of whom were already under economic distress, but the agency itself. She felt an obligation to preserve the health of the organization that played an important role in improving the quality of life for several thousand sick, impoverished, old, and distressed families and individuals, none of whom were ever turned away because of an inability to pay. At least, until a couple of weeks ago. With the economy in a free fall not seen since the Great Depression, this now described almost every client.

Sarah noticed out of the corner of her eye that Sean was amusing himself by flicking spit balls at a social work student who was working at HFS for her field placement, obviously aiming the wads of paper at her chest. She cleared her throat and was about to begin when Sean quipped, "I thought we already decided to paint this room the lavender blue at the last Large Group Intervention meeting."

Sarah pretended to smile, and began her speech. She had rehearsed it several times in front of Harold, but had never felt comfortable. Sarah knew that some of her staff were already preparing updated résumés in expectation that the axe would fall soon.

"As you are aware, there have been rumors about the upcoming board meeting and what actions the board will take to approve a balanced budget for the next fiscal year. The board has directed me to come up with a plan of recommended expense cuts and income enhancements to balance the budget. To this point, no firm decisions have been made, and everything is on the table. The purpose of this meeting is to get some ideas from all of you on how we can achieve what we need to achieve, which, at this point, appears to be a minimum of a 25% retrenchment. This is not good news, and I am not going to sugar-coat what I have to tell you.

"The trends for income are almost universally going south on us and for everyone else who provides social services. Our creditors are hesitant to extend our credit limits because of our shaky cash-flow position, not to mention their own problems with liquidity. Those who owe us money, including several local government agencies and the state, are delaying their reimbursement payments for expenditures we have already incurred on their behalf. We've tried to get a new loan at a rate we could afford, but were unable to do so. Several major donors have reneged on their annual pledges, and you only have to read yesterday's local section of the paper to read why. Our modest endowment, as with virtually every nonprofit organization endowment, has taken a major hit, losing about 40% of its value just in the last year. Many of our clients are either unable to pay upfront for their services or are delaying payment so they can first pay for food, fuel, and medicine."

"How about if we each agree to liberate rolls of toilet paper from public bathrooms, such as movie theaters or at the mall, and bring them here?" Sean offered with a straight face. Sarah simply ignored him.

"Again, everything is on the table. Planned retirements will save us some money if we don't fill replacement positions. We may need to get more aggressive in pursuing some grant opportunities that we avoided in the past because they were not quite consistent with our core mission."

"I had an idea to save money the last time we stayed at a suite at the Marriott for the national conference," Sean said. "If we each took all of our used light bulbs and switched a couple of them for those in the room, and brought them back here, no one would even notice. I guess you can say when I thought of this, the light bulb went on, literally!"

"Sean, this is a serious meeting, and not anything you should make light of," interjected Howie the maintenance man, with a wink. Howie was often Sean's co-conspirator in pulling off some of the more involved practical jokes. Howie was a punster, and in his mind, the more strained the pun, the better. It was once said that "the pun is the lowest form of humor, and poetry is much verse." Even though he was approaching 70 years old, no one could even think of calling Howie "Howard," other than perhaps his mother, who was still alive and living with her cats in Bayonne, N.J.

"Sean, you're not being either helpful or funny," Sarah chided. "Bill, what ideas have you put together for us to think about?"

Bill was the CFO, efficient, a bit nerdy, and the only one in the room who was wearing a suit and tie. Most staff members were wearing their coats, as Sarah two months ago had ordered the thermostat to be turned down to 65 to save on energy costs.

"Well, even if we adopt both of Sean's suggestions, we would still need to close about a million dollars in projected deficit for the current year," he began. "I've considered a few possibilities that would get us closer to where we need to be, but none is without pain. First, we simply have to stop hiring folks to fill the four vacancies that we have been advertising. Second, we can accelerate staff retirements, and offer modest bonuses to those who agree to retire early. We can freeze all training, travel, and conferences—although if we do so, we would lose any potential savings from Sean's suggestions. To avoid layoffs, we can cut hours, like California State government did in 2009, or we might promote job sharing to save on personnel expenses. We can deplete our meager endowment, and perhaps sell off the land we purchased in 2005 for expansion. We could cut salaries and benefits. Lots of organizations already were requiring their employees to pay a higher share of health benefits even before the current economic crisis. We could start using volunteers or non-licensed professionals to handle some of our counseling duties. And, it goes without saying, we need to increase our fees to those who can pay market rates and be more selective about our marketing strategy so that we are not inundated with requests for services that will hemorrhage our resources. Anyway, that is my short list."

"Each of those comes with some costs," interjected Wilma Williams, head of the Social Work Department. Sarah could almost see Wilma's blood pressure rise highlighting the veins in her neck. Sarah worried that her reaction to these trial balloons might trigger a heart event in the heavy-set woman. Wilma, a two-pack-a-day smoker, had been carried away from the room several years earlier after being involved in a heated discussion when HFS was considering making the campus smoke-free. Wilma had threatened to resign on the spot, and then collapsed. She recovered, but Sarah knew that Wilma was not a healthy woman and was on several medications that seemed to affect her vitality that, before that incident, appeared to be almost limitless.

In some respects, Wilma was the glue that kept everything running smoothly, even though she could be abrasive and perhaps too blunt on occasion. "My department is already straining because of the vacancies, and it just isn't fair to my staff or the clients to have caseloads that don't provide the attention required to accomplish what needs to be accomplished. Every one of our social workers is already stretched beyond the breaking point, and we need those four positions filled or we will have more burnout. As for cutting salaries and benefits, that is simply not a viable solution. All of us have bills to pay and families to support. Our staff are highly committed, but it isn't fair to balance our budget on the backs of our employees, who already are making significant financial sacrifices to work here compared to what they could earn in a comparable position in the for-profit sector.

"Yes, it's true that using uncredentialed workers to provide our services would save money. And it would make just as much sense to use a college intern volunteer to be the agency CEO or CFO—it would save money in the short term, but using those without the appropriate education and training to deliver our services or run our agency is penny-wise and pound foolish," she added, clear that she was only just beginning to rant about what she had heard so far.

"And selling off that parcel would have some major negative consequences, as we raised almost a million dollars in some major gifts, making the case that this land would be used for a particular purpose," added Steve Goldman, another social worker who had been with HFS for a decade. "Selling it off would send a wrong signal to these donors and damage our credibility. When the economy improves, we would no longer have this land for our use. In the long term, it would trash our strategic plan, which envisions a major expansion of our campus to accommodate the changing demographics of our community."

Sarah, impressed that anyone on her staff other than herself was familiar with anything in the HFS strategic plan, then asked for other ideas.

"How about being more entrepreneurial, such as by marketing education programs to our middle-class neighborhoods?" offered Kate Johnson, one of the newly-hired social workers who Sarah surmised was quite anxious about whether her job was in jeopardy because of the perception that layoff notices would be meted out based on seniority.

"Excellent suggestion. This is what I am looking for in this meeting," Sarah complimented. "Could you put together a memo for me on this that I could run past the board?"

"We could train our receptionists and other administrative staff to do more hands-on work with clients, and answer our own phones and do our own paperwork, along the lines of reengineering the office to take advantage of technology," offered another social worker. "Whoever answers the phone could pull up information about who is calling, and be empowered to make minor decisions, improving efficiency and avoiding all of the minor interruptions I get when I am meeting with my clients."

"We could explore an effort of reengineering," Sarah said. "Send me a memo outlining how this might work, and which changes might be affordable in the short term."

"We could charge our board members for the lunch and breakfast at the Hilton in three weeks," Sean suggested.

"I don't think so." Sarah responded automatically, although, on further reflection, perhaps this might not be such a bad thing to do.

"Has anyone considered merging with another organization?" offered Steve Hamilton, a staff member who rarely participated in administrative meetings, but was considered to work well with his co-workers and clients. "We could share overhead and perhaps weather the storm."

"Yeah, let's merge with Hooters, and we could get an employee discount for all of us, and add some new services to our therapy department," Sean said. Sarah heard some snickering from the back of the room, but looking at her audience, she saw more annoyance than amusement.

"We could consider a merger down the road, but we are talking more short-term ideas here," Sarah conceded. She turned to Edie Oliver, the Development Director. "Anything you might suggest?"

"Remember back in April when we turned down that six-figure donation from the founder of Ellen Bowman's Boutiques, a couple of months after she was indicted for tax fraud? We might just be desperate enough to see if she still would be willing to make that donation in exchange for naming our building after her. And I'm learning how to conduct on online charitable auction, although even if it is successful, it probably won't make up for the thousands of dollars we won't be getting this year because of poor attendance at our annual tribute dinner."

The suggestion provided fodder for another unwelcome volley from Sean.

"If we are, in principle, willing to sell our good name to the highest bidder, why don't we literally sell our good name and make her an offer to call us the Ellen Bowman Family Service of Harristown for a seven-figure donation? For six figures, we would name our main building after her. And for five figures, we could offer to plaster a decal on the HFS vans that say, "This vehicle sponsored by Ellen, the Felon.""

"And why not have the tribute dinner this year at McDonald's instead of the Hilton, and give everyone a Happy Meal?" Sean said. "We can all collect extra napkins, spoons, forks, and straws for the office lunchroom afterwards. And we could honor Ronald McDonald himself rather than the clown we picked this year."

"Sean," Sarah admonished icily, "That clown is the board chair of this organization, my boss, and at least for the moment, your boss, as well." Everyone laughed, other than Sean, who got the message and shrunk back into his seat, wounded.

Sarah spent the next 15 minutes fielding more suggestions, tried to mask how disheartened she was by the responses, and then brought the meeting to a close.

"Thank you for all of your suggestions," she said, the cue that the meeting was over. "We will reconvene after the board meeting, and I will share what decisions the board makes with respect to these issues."

As people filed out, some looking shell-shocked and some angry or scared, one of the fluorescent lights began to flicker. *Maybe Sean's light bulb idea isn't such a bad suggestion, after all,* she mused.

Discussion Questions

1. Make a list of the serious suggestions made for increasing income and cutting expenses mentioned in this meeting. What are the benefits and limitations of each?

2. Had you been in this meeting, what other suggestions might you have offered?

3. For the most part, Sarah handled Sean's inappropriate comments by simply ignoring him. What message did that send to the others in the meeting? How would you have handled someone like Sean?

4. Was it appropriate to have every staff member in the room to discuss what strategies might be employed to close the budget deficit? What are the costs and benefits of doing this rather than simply having professional staff hammer out the recommendations it will make to the board?

5. When an organization is in crisis, how much information should be shared with all staff members who might be affected by management decisions? Under what conditions might it be considered ethical for organizational leadership not to be completely honest with staff?

6. What are the pros and cons of HFS considering applying for grants that are "not quite consistent with our core mission"?

7. Discuss the costs and benefits of accepting or seeking donations from convicted felons.

Case 4

HHA's Dilemma: Be a Good Citizen or Fight Extortion

Deborah Williams, the CEO and President of the non-profit Harristown Home for the Aged, responded to the knock on the door of her office with a "Come in, Steve," recognizing the distinctive knock of her CFO.

"This is not good," began Steve Rightgold, his usually deadpan face betraying signs of the anxiety he was feeling about the news he was about to relay to his boss. He brandished a single piece of paper and thrust it out to Deborah.

She skimmed it and let out an audible groan. "Not what we need now," she told him.

For nearly a decade, Steve had competently kept financial operations running smoothly in a complex environment that required the constant juggling of nearly a dozen different accounts to maintain a positive cash flow situation for the facility. In recent months, accomplishing this successfully had become more of a struggle. With budget cuts beginning to be implemented by the State's Medicaid program and with many of the home's private pay residents falling behind on paying their invoices, HHA was already in financial distress, as were virtually all of its competitors, nonprofit and for-profit alike. In theory, HHA was a charity, exempt from federal income taxes under Section 501(c)(3) of the Internal Revenue Code, and also exempt from paying local property taxes levied by the county, city of Harristown, and the Harristown School District.

The reality, as Ms. Williams was often reminded, was that HHA doled out only a minimum level of charity to the needy. And by any calculation, that amount was usually less than that provided by most of the for-profit competitors in her community.

Perhaps at one time in its early history, in the early 20th century, HHA had operated like a traditional charity, considering itself to be an old-age home, accepting residents who had no place else to go regardless of whether they needed health care. Back then, there was no continuum of long-term care that ranged from designated long-term care wings of acute care hospitals at one end of the spectrum to providing services in the home to those who could maintain their independence. HHA had participated in providing services to almost this entire range, including providing services to those in what have been designated as Naturally Occurring Retirement Communities (NORCs), funded by grants authorized by the 2006 revision of the *Older Americans Act.*

NORCs are geographical areas with a high concentration of older persons who have "aged in place," in housing not originally intended for an elderly population. Deborah had personally visited one member of the community who was still independent in her home at the age of 95, and who received chore services. She could still drive to the supermarket by herself, but she was unable to replace a burned-out light bulb in her ceiling by herself. "Not quite as spry as I used to be," the woman had admitted to her.

In between those two poles are a wide range of services that are available to the aged, offering various degrees of independence. With the fastest growing age group in the county (and the country, as well) the over-85 cohort, long-term care had come a long way since being 60 was considered "old" and folks were shipped off to nursing homes to die and be out of the way.

At one end of the continuum of long-term care are services available to those who can stay in their own homes such as chore services; senior centers such as those sponsored by Area Agencies on Aging (AAA); home health care provided by visiting nurses; respite care programs provided in the home; and adult day care programs whereby seniors travel to a central site during the day to receive healthcare, recreation, and peer companionship. HHA participated in several such programs, and even made a profit, which was used to cover the difference between costs and revenue it received from the Medicaid program for traditional nursing home care services.

Aging individuals who required minimal health interventions might leave their residences for housing designated for the aged, such as retirement housing communities and continuing care retirement communities. Those choosing the latter service might sign a contract that guaranteed their admission to a skilled nursing facility should their deteriorating health conditions require it.

Aged individuals who were relatively healthy but required some assistance in performing activities of daily living such as eating and bathing might opt for an assisted living facility, which also had medical staff on site and on call.

HHA had expanded its campus several years earlier by purchasing an adjacent parcel for the purpose of building an assisted living facility, which was projected by a marketing study to make a net revenue contribution to HHA. Unfortunately, HHA made its land purchase from a for-profit corporation that had paid substantial real estate taxes to the city and county.

Perhaps it was this that had triggered the letter from the County addressed to Steve, although it was quite possible that every charitable long-term care facility in the county had been a recipient of one like it. Deborah would have to find out. And the most intensive long-term care short of hospitalization was the nursing home that offered both skilled and intermediate care, the main business and focus of HHA. The facility she ran had 120 beds, with only a handful of vacancies at any one time.

Deborah was in constant competition with other facilities for filling those beds with aging individuals who could pay the private pay rate as long as possible before converting to Medicaid, which increasingly reimbursed the home for a large, but declining share of its actual expenses. But one couldn't survive by keeping too many beds vacant in the hope that a call would come from a well-heeled client with the ability to afford the private pay rate and with enough health problems to justify admission.

Deborah mused that almost all of her residents had enough medical problems that would have required treatment in an acute care hospital only a few decades earlier. And many residents in her home had been admitted directly from such a hospital, often still seriously ill, but discharged simply because their insurance payments would no longer justify keeping them hospitalized. "Quicker and sicker" was the cliché used to describe the realities of managed care. In most cases, Medicare rather than Medicaid would reimburse the home for short stays for those who were admitted to the home directly from a hospital, and at least so far, Medicare reimbursements were reasonable.

Still, Deborah was proud that her facility could boast that some residents improved enough as a result of the services she provided with a committed staff that they could return to their homes after a few weeks or months at HHA. And those residents who died while in the facility's care did so with dignity.

For perhaps a couple of decades, nursing home residents needed to be certified by the state as having serious health problems that justified their being cared for in that facility—and those problems might well have been more appropriate to be dealt with in a hospital just a few decades earlier. Today's modern nursing home bore little resemblance to that of the 1960s, let alone that of the 1920s. Each resident, for example, required an average of 2-3 hours of care by licensed nurses, and many residents had serious health needs that required physician services. A new philosophy was that residents in nursing homes could receive and benefit from rehabilitation services and could improve their health status as a result of being in the facility, rather than simply being warehoused there until they died. And with this new philosophy came a concurrent increase in the expenses of these services.

As a practical matter, no modern reasonably-sized long-term care facility could afford to provide free services to more than one or two residents, if that, with verifiable costs approaching $70,000 annually for the residents who required the least amount of care. HHA also cared for residents on ventilators and had an Alzheimer's wing, and costs for care in those units were astronomical.

Typically, almost every resident admitted to HHA came there as a private-pay resident, paying the full market rate of $6,000 per month. They would spend down their assets and then be added to the Medicaid program, a federal-state partnership that financed long-term care and many other health care services for the indigent. Ironically, few residents at HHA whose expensive health care was being financed by federal and state taxpayers were "poor." Rather, they were almost all from middle-class backgrounds and had either spent down their life savings before converting to Medicaid or had found a legal way to transfer their assets to family members. Many of these family members were upper middle- or middle-class themselves and could afford to contribute to the health care costs of their aging and ill family member if government policy so provided.

Deborah reached across her desk and started reading the letter from the beginning, word for word. The letter was from the Alford County Board of Assessment Appeals. In a terse, three paragraph letter, the head of the board noted that the board determined that the parcel on which the HHA was located did not qualify for tax-exempt status because the home didn't meet the board's interpretation of the statutory test for community benefit for charities provided exemption from county real estate taxes. HHA owed the county for back real estate taxes for each of the previous three years.

"And the bad news is that the same criteria for exemption are used to determine local property taxes, which have a liability of several times what the county wants from us," Steve informed her. "This could easily cost us six figures, unless we find some way to deal with this."

All of this was vaguely familiar to Deborah. Back in the 1980s, she had been the chief financial officer at another nursing home in the state and had received a similar letter. She remembered that the County solicitor had sent the form letter to virtually every tax-exempt charity with property in the county, referencing some court cases that had been decided that revoked the tax-exemptions of a hospital and nursing home. Economic conditions back then mirrored what was occurring today: High unemployment, a burgeoning increase in the demand for services, a decline of the taxable tax base as tax-exempt charities expanded their real estate holdings, draconian cuts of state and federal grants to local governments, and unfunded mandates. Many cities had suffered an erosion of their tax base as wealthy residents sought to improve their quality of life by fleeing the explosion of drug abuse, crime, homelessness, deteriorating public education systems, and other city ills to the perceived safety and security of the suburbs.

Some, but not all, local governments responded with a powerful weapon—threaten well-heeled charities with the loss of their tax exemption unless they agreed to pony up millions of dollars in PILOTs (payments-in-lieu-of-taxes).

At the time, Deborah's facility had considered the letter to be a thinly disguised extortion plot—either agree to make payments to the local government or face the inevitability of incurring hundreds of thousands of dollars in legal fees to fight the battle in court. The board of Deborah's facility had made the decision to make a settlement with the county and local governments, which siphoned off over a million dollars over the course of 10 years that would have otherwise been available to provide services. She remembered the board had had an internal struggle that frayed relationships for years afterwards, as about half of the members wanted to fight the tax challenge as a simple matter of standing up to injustice and the other half were more pragmatic. Even then, Deborah had had some ambivalence herself about how the board should have responded.

She knew that her previous facility, while it did provide substantial services to the poor and admitted residents who required subsidization at the time of their admission, did so because of its affiliation with a religious order that bent over backwards to make its services accessible to those in need, and diverted hundreds of thousands of donated dollars for that purpose. HHA was not structured that way, and would have a difficult, but not impossible, task proving that it did provide a substantial amount of charitable services. But, on the other hand, she had to admit to herself that her previous facility did require county and city services, such as police and fire protection, and was in a stable enough financial position to make a contribution toward funding these services at a time when all local governments were distressed.

Now, the situation was different. Although the distress of the local governments was real and serious, almost all nonprofit long-term care facilities were equally distressed. Reimbursements for care provided by the federal and state governments were being cut. Deborah knew that every time the fire alarm was pulled, either for a fire or a false alarm, at least three emergency vehicles would respond immediately, and more would follow if there was an actual fire. The county road that ran adjacent to the facility was plowed shortly after snowstorms. She would have been quick to acknowledge that the facility benefited from the services of local government.

On the other hand, the county ran a nursing home itself, and Deborah justified that by serving needy clients, she was relieving the government of a burden. Taxing the facility would simply mean that fewer residents would be able to be subsidized.

One of her board members, Jane Udall, a prominent attorney with both personal and professional ties to the county commissioners, might be able to shed some light on the situation. With one telephone call, Deborah knew she could get a better picture as to the extent to which the County had spread its net to try to capture revenue.

She was grateful that the receptionist put her right through to Jane.

"Let me apologize for not giving you a heads up on this," Jane told her, "but what I knew about this was required to be confidential, and I honored that. But now that the cat is out of the bag, I can answer any questions you might have, at least to the extent that I know about this."

Deborah wasted no time getting to the point. "How is this going to play out, what is our exposure, and what can we do about it?"

Jane, cognizant that she was "not on the clock" generating the legal fees she needed that justified her status as a senior partner of the firm, came right to the point.

"There are two aspects of this," she began. "The legal issues and the political issues. The legal issues are a bit complicated, but I can summarize them quickly.

"The State Constitution authorizes the legislature to statutorily grant tax exemptions. It did so years ago. In the 1980s, some local governments, including ours, were suffering economically, and decided to challenge whether tax-exempt charities met the Constitutional and statutory criteria. At the time, it was somewhat of a 'Hail Mary' effort. But to the surprise of many, some courts agreed with the local governments, and interpreted (most say 'misinterpreted') previous court decisions on this. Lots of large hospitals and nursing homes, and other types of facilities, even the YMCAs, lost their cases, and many others simply agreed to make PILOTs to avoid the prospect of losing their tax-exemptions altogether or having to pay hundreds of thousands of dollars in legal fees to protect them. Eventually, the charitable community organized, convinced the Legislature to pass a law protecting exemptions, and also benefited from a couple of cases that went up to the State Supreme Court. And by the time all this occurred, the economy had improved, and local governments were no longer desperate for the money.

"Now for the politics of this. Generally, the county commissioners have reached the obvious conclusion that they are facing a massive budget deficit unless they either cut spending or increase income. They were willing to absorb the political fallout when they cut library spending almost in half last year, and started phasing out some lucrative, but wasteful, consulting contracts that were politically expedient for the majority commissioners. This year, there is not as much wiggle room to cut any waste, and certainly no interest in raising taxes, particularly in an election year. That is just not going to happen. The feds have quietly cut a lot of grants that go directly to counties in the last couple of years. So, what they decided to do—at least the two majority commissioners with the tacit assent of the third—is to send these letters to every hospital and nursing home in the county. The thinking is that a lot of these facilities have lots of cash stashed away for emergencies. And many of them, particularly the hospitals, are perceived as pretending to hide behind their charitable exemptions while in practice engaging in as little charity as they can get away with.

"Back in the 1980s, when the county did something like this, half of our hospitals agreed to provide payments-in-lieu-of-taxes that funneled millions of dollars to the county coffers over the ten-year period of the agreement. I don't remember any of those hospitals suffering from this.

"My guess is that HHA might be better off making contacts with the majority on the commission and work out a PILOT deal on favorable terms. That is basically what they are looking for, as engaging in litigation is not only expensive for those who receive these letters, but also for the county, as well. I would expect the county commissioners would be sympathetic about the ability of HHA to pay, and HHA would probably have to pay less for a PILOT agreement than it would if the case went to court and HHA had to pay for legal fees, even if it won. Normally, I would expect my firm would pledge to do some of this *pro bono,* but we also have the county as our client, so we would be unable to participate directly in helping you out, as we have done in the past because of the conflict of interest we would have in representing both parties. But from what I can tell, the real target of these letters is the hospitals, and you and the other nursing homes are going along for the ride, along with some other facilities in the county that are perceived to have lots of revenue, require lots of county services, and are perceived to offer minimal amounts of free services to the needy."

"I think I understand," Deborah responded. "What options do we have?"

"Well, this situation is similar to what happened in the 1980s. Some charities fought the challenges in court. Eventually, one of these cases from another county worked its way up to the state's Supreme Court, and the charities won a victory that effectively ended the litigation.

"Some waved the white flag and worked out a deal with the local governments to provide payments-in-lieu-of-taxes on favorable terms, often negotiating the provision of providing more free and subsidized services than they were previously providing. At the time, I was a young lawyer in town and I was engaged in negotiating a couple of these agreements. One thing I remember that was helpful was that my client put together a detailed audit of all of the charity it provided, including the value of all of the volunteer work contributed. The facility also quantified how the amount reimbursed under the Medicaid program did not cover all of its costs.

"And I would recommend that while you and the board are deciding between these two options, HHA can participate in an organized effort by those in HAA's situation to work out a county-wide settlement with the other side, or organize a statewide advocacy effort to protect charities from efforts such as this. If the legislature came up with some money to pay to local governments that agree not to challenge the exemptions of these facilities, the local governments would put the dogs back on the leash."

"Thanks, Jane. You've been helpful, as always. I'll see you at the board meeting."

Deborah hung up and considered the recommendation she would make to her board at its next meeting the following month.

Discussion Questions:

1. Discuss the pros and cons of negotiating a PILOT agreement with the county and the alternative option of mounting a legal defense to the tax challenge.

2. What are some of the steps Deborah should take if she chooses to engage in helping to organize other facilities to respond to these letters?

3. Discuss some of the politics of engaging in a fight among those who are usually natural allies, such as those who have close ties to local government and those with close ties to charities.

4. Discuss how fair it is that the Medicaid long-term care program finances care mostly to those who were not needy at any point during their healthy lives.

5. Research laws relating to how one qualifies for the Medicaid program. Discuss the ethics of whether it is fair that wealthy children of Medicaid-eligible persons are not required to make any contribution to the care of their parents, and what may be legally done by nursing home residents to protect substantial assets so that they can qualify for having the government pay their costs of care.

6. Nonprofit nursing homes often point to the fact that Medicaid fails to pay the full cost of care for residents in these beds, and thus these homes contribute millions of dollars in charity care to make up the difference. Those who manage for-profit homes can say that they also have a substantial number of residents who are cared for under Medicaid (in some states, even more than nonprofit homes), and they provide this care without any real estate exemption. Discuss the validity of both perspectives.

7. Discuss whether the same rules with respect to tax exemptions should apply to hospitals, nursing homes, and other "commercial" nonprofits that will typically charge a market rate for their services compared to charities that do not charge clients for services, or that charge a modest amount.

Case 5

Museum and Historical Association State Budget Cuts

"It's Kevin on line 2," chirped Betty on Louise Wilson's intercom.

Louise Wilson was the executive director of the State Historical and Museum Association, a four-employee nonprofit organization. Betty was the bookkeeper and administrative assistant who did double duty by answering the telephones. Kevin Peters, calling in from the State Capitol, was the communications and government relations professional. The only other employee of the association, Bill Stevens, was an historian who had museum management experience with a large art museum in Philadelphia.

While Louise spent most of her time keeping her 15-member board happy and working with the consultant fundraiser, Bill provided management and other technical assistance to the 67 museums and historical associations that were dues-paying members. In addition to being the association's registered lobbyist, Kevin also maintained the organization's Web site, produced the monthly newsletter, and issued press releases.

All four employees, along with a small cadre of committed volunteers and an occasional summer intern, participated in planning fundraisers, preparing for board meetings, and sorting the bulk mail for the newsletters. Some services, such as the bulk mail tasks for the newsletter and fundraising, previously had been outsourced. A reflection of the economic times, the budget of the Association had eroded steadily in recent years, as its membership had experienced a hemorrhage of income losses and an increase in expenses. Museum visits not only statewide but nationwide, as well, had suffered a steady decline over several decades, victim to a change in the way children and adults alike spent their leisure time. It was tough enough to compete with movie theaters and television. Adding the lure and addiction of the Internet and video games exacerbated the competition.

Although many museums had a loyal following, it was difficult to keep the Association's membership able to finance fresh exhibits that would encourage return visitors. As membership had dwindled and government subsidies had evaporated, many museums found it necessary to raise their admission fees, which fed into the cycle of declining membership.

During the latest economic turmoil, arts and education related nonprofits had suffered disproportionately from budget cuts from government, as well as cuts in grants from foundation funders. Few museums could boast of any sizeable endowments, and even those that were able to divert endowment funding to cover operational deficits recognized that it was only a temporary measure. All arts organizations and museums were at risk from a plethora of challenging crises. Energy costs had gone through the roof (literally, for those that did not have any weatherization program). This not only fattened the heating and cooling bills of facilities, but also affected the willingness of patrons to get in their cars and travel to a museum when they could stay in their homes and download a pay-on-demand movie through their cable boxes. Costs for security and insurance had skyrocketed, along with the cost of health insurance and other employee benefits. And there was nothing on the horizon that promised any relief.

Louise, herself, was often stressed out from the increasing workload. This was not fair. But it was also not a good time to be seeking another job, particularly in this field, which was clearly declining. She remembered that several years earlier, one of her board members had approached her about joining his firm as a manager in the financial services industry at a starting salary that had dwarfed her own. After a long discussion with her husband, she had decided to rebuff the offer, knowing that her heart was in the work she was doing. Whenever she had received the tuition bills from her son's college, she had thought wistfully about the wisdom of her decision. Ironically, that board member was now unemployed after his firm had gone belly up only months before it might have benefited from federal bailout legislation promoted by an outgoing President Bush and an incoming President Obama.

Kevin waited patiently as Louise braced herself and took the call.

"Good news or bad?" Louise asked, as she picked up the telephone. Most news she had received lately had been bad, as reliable funders had dropped out with hardly a warning. Several large institutional members had indicated to her that they might need to defer this year's dues payments to her and other associations and coalitions that they participated in to avoid laying off even more employees. At one time during the high-flying economic boom of the 1990s, the Association had employed six full-time and a couple of part-time employees. A failing economy and the loss of revenue had necessitated a slow retrenchment of spending by the Association. Two long-time employees, both of whom had been employed since its founding in 1975, had retired and were not replaced. Their duties had been absorbed by other staff.

The residual stress accruing to the organization from this response had its consequences. Louise knew that both Betty and Bill were looking for other jobs. It was not that they were disloyal; Louise conceded that she was requiring them to devote more time to the organization than they could reasonably be expected to sustain for much longer.

"Well, would you rather have the bad news first, or the really bad news?" Kevin responded. Kevin had spent most of the morning and half of the afternoon at the Capitol Building, listening to the Governor's budget address and obtaining a hard copy of the budget proposal. All of the numbers would be posted online later in the day, but as a state association executive, Louise knew that one of her most critically important tasks was to provide information about developments to her membership as soon as possible. Nothing annoyed her more than one of her members finding out some juicy piece of information about state government from a source other than the Association.

Kevin was good at his job. He would tell her what she needed to know without any equivocation, and he knew that she would not shoot the messenger.

Louise was somewhat prepared for bad news from the Governor, who had a public face as a fiscal conservative, but who had a soft spot in his heart for funding programs that improved the quality of life for his state's citizens, such as the arts, humanities, museums, and programs that improved the health care and education of children. The Governor, an affable, congenial man who made those around him comfortable, had four children and 12 grandchildren, which some said had a great influence on his public policy. Others attributed this warm spot he had for the arts and humanities to the fact that the State's First Lady had been a librarian, and was a *sub rosa* advocate for programs that were not traditionally embraced by self-proclaimed fiscal conservatives. But having met the Governor a couple of times at ground-breaking ceremonies, Louise judged that he was a sincere supporter of museums and the educational role they play in increasing the social capital of a community.

"I already expect it will be bad," Louise responded, "and the draft Action Alert you prepared for distribution today to the membership about the budget wasn't very optimistic. How much do we need to change it? If I remember, we estimated a 20% cut in the line-item for museums and historical associations."

"Well, I hope you are sitting down," Kevin began his report via cell phone. "The bad news is that the Governor zeroed out our line-item entirely."

"Ouch, what could be the really bad news, then?" she replied as calmly as she could, although she felt the blood rush to her head.

For a moment, she relived the feeling she had felt in February of 2009 when she read about a highly prestigious art museum in Nevada, the Las Vegas Art Museum, simply closing its doors with only a few days of public notice. At the time, many other nationally respected institutions, including the Philadelphia Museum of Art and Atlanta's High Museum of Art, had announced severe layoffs in addition to other budget-cutting measures, but it was the emerging story in Las Vegas that had traumatized those in the "industry." A couple of months before it had summarily closed, the board of the Las Vegas institution had instituted draconian measures intended to save the organization, which was projecting an unacceptable budget deficit. The executive director there had responded by announcing her resignation.

The Las Vegas museum had received only 3% of its budget from government funding, and at the time it had closed, membership had dwindled to only 1,000 individuals. Louise knew full well that many of her members depended on state funds for substantially more than 3% of their income. For a moment, she envisioned "Closed to the Public" signs on the front doors of constituent institutions of the Association. Unthinkable for something like that to happen on her watch!

"The Guv also zeroed out all of the earmarked grants that our members receive, including the $1 million for Harristown," Kevin said. Harristown was the Harristown Art Museum (HAM), the largest and most prestigious art museum in the state, which provided the Association with almost 25% of its annual budget. The current chair of the board of the Association was Dr. Elizabeth Bowman, the crusty executive director of HAM. She would not be happy, and unlike Louise, the "lizard," as Elizabeth was called behind her back, might indeed shoot the messenger who delivered bad tidings.

"The Guv basically said that he will do everything in his power not to raise taxes and to protect every existing service the state funds that directly protects the health, safety, and welfare of the state's citizens. He not only zeroed us out, but he also zeroed out state supplemental funds to libraries, subsidies to parks, the state's athletic programs, and the senior citizen public transportation program. And that might be the really bad news, as the General Assembly will do whatever it takes to find funds to restore the senior transportation program, for the obvious reasons."

"What else can you tell me?" Louise prodded, holding on to her desk for support, and trying not to convey the panic that she increasingly was feeling at the moment.

"Well, I had a minute to chat with Stevens, the House Majority Whip and Williamson, the Senate Minority Leader. Both are sympathetic to restoring some of the money, and both seem to think the Governor cut us to the bone knowing full well that the Legislature would put back some money, so he could present a balanced budget. He probably won't oppose putting all or some of our money back unless it takes something away from some other program he supports more. The problem is that the money has to be found somewhere, and most of the money the legislature had hidden away for purposes such as this were dug up from their hiding places last year when the libraries were the target of budget cuts." He paused a moment. "And, of course, no one is suggesting raising taxes."

Louise considered this for a moment before responding. "I remember that a nephew of the Senate Minority Leader is a curator for Harristown, and is located in the district of the House Majority Leader, who usually protects their interests. How did this happen to Harristown?"

"I don't know for sure, but I think this may be some payback for Williamson leading the veto override fight on the Governor's pet health care reform plan," Kevin responded. "Look, I am still in shock about this myself. I am a bit blindsided by this, and I would have expected that my friends in the Front Office would have given me a heads up." The "Front Office" was the term Kevin and other lobbyists used to describe the Governor's Office.

"The Governor throws stones at the frogs in sport, but the frogs die not in sport but in earnest," Louise mused, para-phrasing Plutarch, more to herself than to Kevin. "So, come back here as soon as you can. I need to talk to the Lizard about what we can tell the board and what we can tell the general membership about this," Louise commanded. "I guess the only good news is that this budget is only a recommenda-tion, and we have four months before the budget deadline to convince our friends in the Legislature that these draconian cuts simply aren't fair. And we have to send out the Action Alert ASAP."

Louise hung up the telephone, closed the door to her office, and took a deep breath. Although none of the funds the state made available in the Museum and Historical Com-mission line-item came to the Association directly, there was a general agreement among the board and its members that dues to the Association were based in large part on the state funding the Association was able to obtain. For the past sev-eral years, the line-item had received a perfunctory 2-3% cost-of-living increase, along with other line-items that did not have high visibility or a politically powerful constituency, such as programs for the aged, basic education, or subsidies for colleges and universities.

In her heart, Louise had feared that the 20% cut in funding might become reality, but the news from Kevin was far worse than even her worst-case scenario. Being zeroed out was unfathomable. She judged that the Association and its allies had enough political influence to restore some of the funds, but was it realistic to think that it was possible to get all of the money restored? Even getting the line-item restored to its funding from the previous year was a *de facto* cut, as inflation eroded the value of each dollar of revenue.

Louise pulled up a database on her computer that tracked political contributions made to the leadership of the State Legislature and Governor by friends and stakeholders of the Association. Impressive as it was, the current budget situation could very well trump this aspect of the Association's power. At least, it helped Kevin get access to the movers and shakers in the Capitol to make the Association's case one-on-one. But compared to the access provided by the telecommunications, trial lawyer, and the insurance lobbies, the influence of the entire nonprofit sector was minimal. The good news was that many individuals on Louise's list were associated one way or the other with the powerful organizations that really ran state government. Hopefully, they could be convinced to help.

Louise knew that whereas Kevin was good at providing data and convincing arguments, public policy made in the Governor's Mansion and the halls of the Capitol emanated more on the golf course and at $500 per plate fundraisers. Few nonprofit associations or organizations had the resources to invest in this game, and those that did represented the interests of hospitals and institutions of higher learning—certainly not museums and historical societies. Louise took it as a given that Harristown University's state subsidy was safe from the sharp knives of state budget cutters, partly because legislative leaders and the Governor had access to a private sky box for every home game.

It occurred to Louise that the museums would have some natural allies with which to align themselves and marshal a public outcry. She took out a legal pad and started writing changes to the text of the Action Alert that would be e-mailed that afternoon with the bad news. Included in her draft was a pledge that she would do everything in her power to restore the funds, and that every stakeholder needed to pitch in to help with the coordinated advocacy effort that would be required.

As she looked down at her legal pad, she smiled through the tears.

Discussion Questions:

1. What arguments might Louise and her allies make that the state needs to support programs other than those that directly protect the health, safety, and welfare of the state's citizens? If Louise wrote an Op-Ed article about it, what arguments might she make?

2. What are some of the advocacy activities the Association might engage in to help the cause?

3. Do you think Louise has the resources to start and build a successful coalition to restore these cuts? Could she afford not to? Discuss who might be natural coalition partners, and who might be better avoided.

4. What is the author referring to when he uses the term "social capital," and why is this considered an important concept in the study of nonprofit management?

5. How much influence do you think personal experience of public officials (such as firsthand contact with relatives who have a disease or a particular disability) has on the execution of public policy compared to general ideology? Is it ever inappropriate to exploit the knowledge of that experience? How might that be done in this particular case?

6. What is the role of the board in helping to restore funding to the Association's membership?

7. Is it unethical for public policymakers to take advantage of the private skybox offered by Harristown University at home football games? Why or why not?

Case 6

Evaluating Dr. Luddite, Harristown Asperger's Syndrome Foundation Executive Director

Tempers were beginning to flare at the mid-August board meeting of the Harristown Asperger's Syndrome Foundation, and the atmosphere was hot enough as it was. The air conditioner had been turned down in the conference room to save on cooling expenses and satisfy a "green agenda" advanced by a coalition of nonprofits of which the Foundation was a member. The board was split right down the middle on whether to fire its long-time executive director, an action that the chair of the Foundation and convener of the meeting, Stephen Huddleston III, had considered to be inconceivable only hours ago.

"Dr. Luddite should retire gracefully," brusquely accused Ryan Powers, a 30-something investment banker with an MBA who had little patience for beating around the bush. He had been the one a half-hour previously to offer the motion not to renew Dr. Luddite's contract, effectively firing him on December 31.

"Absolutely," agreed Tom Davies, the only "Generation Z" member of the board and only a few years out of college himself. "He should step aside and let a younger person with fresh ideas and experience in running a modern nonprofit bring the Foundation into the 21st century. Or at least the 20th century," he added pointedly, thinking he was being funny.

Powers and Davies had been a tag team, taking turns at battering the executive director without any indication that they would ever run out of ammunition against him. It might take some fancy footwork along with some parliamentary maneuvering for the CEO's defenders to deflect their frontal attack and provide enough acknowledgment of their complaints to placate them and other disgruntled board members. What would it take to convince them to withdraw their motion and substitute something more constructive and more in the interests of the Foundation? Even if their motion carried,

Huddleston was confident that he could muster a re-vote on the action by having another meeting before December 31 with the attendance of some of the board members who were absent today. But it would take a major effort to smooth ruffled feathers, and who knows how Dr. Luddite would interpret the board's current debate once it leaked out to him what was occurring, as it inevitably would.

"I don't think either of you appreciates how much Dr. Luddite means to this organization," parried Ruth Winnett. She was one of the original board members of the organization and among the legions of individuals who worshipped Dr. Luddite and raved about his accomplishments on behalf of those like her who had a child with Asperger's Syndrome.

"This organization would never be able to replace him if he decided to leave voluntarily, and it would be a disaster to fire him, not to mention how unfair it would be to him. He has devoted his entire professional life to our cause, and we should be judging him on the results of his efforts, not the specific management techniques that he uses. I think we would be better served if both of you left the board if you're not happy, rather than having Dr. Luddite leave."

"Okay, let's get back to focusing on the Personnel Committee's executive director evaluation recommendations and the motion on the floor," implored Mr. Huddleston.

Mr. Huddleston surveyed the conference room one more time, looking for any sign that the 16 members of the Harristown Asperger's Foundation board before him would reach a consensus on the future of its long-time executive director and organizational co-founder. *We should have found some way to throw at least three of these folks off the board last year before it got to this, and perhaps I deserve some of the blame for letting things deteriorate to the point they have,* he admitted to himself.

The main agenda item was what was expected to be a perfunctory approval of the formal annual executive director evaluation report of the Personnel Committee. The committee, which was appointed by the chair, had generally agreed that Dr. Luddite's performance was exemplary, but he could improve the management of the Foundation by infusing some technological innovation into its operations.

But things were getting out of control at this meeting. Some renegade members of the board were using the discussion of the report to express their dissatisfaction with the organization's leadership in general, and the quality of the leadership of Dr. Michael Luddite, in particular. Chair Huddleston was irritated; this was the type of situation that needed to be diffused before it reached the board meeting stage. As a courtesy, Mr. Powers, the apparent leader of the cabal engaged in trashing Luddite, could have at least given the chair a heads-up that there was going to be a challenge of some kind. The debate did not appear to be spontaneous with Powers, Davies, and two others speaking out against retaining Dr. Luddite.

Now in the last year of his two-year term as chair, Mr. Huddleston had accepted the position by unanimous vote, and he had helped guide the organization through some turbulent economic times. He had forged a good relationship with Michael Luddite, Ph.D., the CEO and an icon in the social service community for nearly a half-century, who worked tirelessly for children with Asperger's and the families who cared for them. Putting aside the substantial discomfort that would accrue to the organization by firing Dr. Luddite, Huddleston knew that a search for a replacement executive director would consume significant time and resources of the Foundation (and those of himself, personally), and that it would be unlikely for the organization to find someone of Dr. Luddite's experience and national stature.

In 1995, the Luddites' eight-year-old grandson had been diagnosed with Asperger's after a frustrating three-year search for the cause of his often baffling behavior. At the time, Dr. Luddite had been the long-serving director of the State's Medicaid program, serving a succession of Republican and Democratic Governors and their politically appointed Secretaries of Health and Human Services. For almost three decades, none had given even a thought to replacing Dr. Luddite, as was routinely the case with all other deputy secretaries in the department. He was a nationally respected expert on many aspects of the program, and his résumé documented his vast experience over the years advising presidential commissions, the National Governors Association, and others who were influential in shaping public policy in that area.

That same year, Dr. Luddite had been abruptly fired over his unwillingness to implement certain cost containment policies demanded by the Governor's Office. Rather than retiring on his substantial state pension, as many in his position might have done, Luddite instead engaged in a Herculean effort to organize a coalition of parents and health care providers focused on Asperger's. Both he and his wife, a registered nurse, had devoted the next 15 years to advocacy at the state and federal levels to find effective treatments if not an outright cure, provide government support for providing services to families with the syndrome, and educate the professional health community and the public about it.

Asperger's Syndrome (a.k.a. Asperger's Disorder, or Asperger's) is a behavioral syndrome associated with autism that affects approximately one in every 5,000 children in the United States and around the globe—although epidemiological studies to gauge its prevalence have varied widely. Its name derives from Hans Asperger, the Austrian medical doctor who in 1944 was the first to catalog its symptoms—an impairment in non-verbal communication, physical clumsiness, and limitations empathizing with others. It had taken another half-century before Asperger's had become a standard diagnosis, a delay that had caused immense grief and suffering to the families of children with the syndrome, who often suffered through the frustrations of misdiagnoses. There is no known single cause, although a genetic link has been established. There is also no reliable treatment; rather the symptoms are managed by behavioral therapy. Those who also suffer from depression and anxiety—which are not unusual to accompany Asperger's—receive medications targeted to relieving those particular symptoms. In recent years, autism, ADD, and ADHD had become well known nationally as a result of extensive media interest. Asperger's Disorder was less well-known, though certainly more known as a result of the work of Dr. Luddite and the Foundation.

As with other behavioral disorders in children, such as ADHD, Asperger's is both over-diagnosed and under-diagnosed, partly attributable to the fact that there is a wide spectrum of the syndrome's degree of severity. The Foundation had dedicated much of its efforts to assuring that the health care community received the education it needed to appropriately diagnose the syndrome, and had been one of the leading organizations to assist in the development of screening instruments.

As it was, Dr. Luddite was not present, as he was traveling across the country to help organize a parallel foundation in another state. He would not have been in the room while his evaluation was being discussed, but it might have helped if he had been accessible to answer questions. For most nonprofit executive directors, being on the opposite coast would not be a major obstacle. The fact that Dr. Luddite was unreachable during this crisis only underscored the point his detractors were making.

The Foundation was Luddite's vision from the beginning. He and a small group of parents and grandparents had incorporated the Foundation, and they seeded its operations from their personal funds. At first, there had been no paid staff, and Dr. Luddite had chaired the board and voluntarily, with the assistance of his wife, managed the Foundation. After only two years, a well-heeled member had bankrolled the organization with a small six-figure contribution with promises to renew the gift annually. At that point, Dr. Luddite decided to become the organization's executive director and continue to serve on the board in a non-voting, *ex officio* capacity. Mrs. Luddite had continued to serve on the board and served as its chair until her death in 2002.

Initially, Dr. Luddite suffered through a severe case of founder's syndrome. This term has been used to describe situations in which the founder of an organization dominates decisionmaking through his or her commitment, passion, or personal charisma. This dominance eventually becomes inappropriate behavior as the organization matures and governance and management become more decentralized through a group of diverse stakeholders. But in time, he became more comfortable with the more restricted role of CEO. Helping him through this often painful process was an outside consultant hired to develop a five-year strategic plan for the foundation. Eventually, Dr. Luddite and the board recognized that it was Dr. Luddite's job to manage, and the board's job to govern. In time, Dr. Luddite had accepted this division of responsibility.

Dr. Luddite was always respectful of board members, but it was not unusual for him to ignore the board's directions on occasion, particularly when he perceived that the board had overstepped its authority and was inappropriately micromanaging. For example, back in 2007, the board had passed a resolution, offered by the organization's treasurer, directing Dr. Luddite to invest the Foundation's entire available bank account with Bernie Madoff, a former chairman of the Nasdaq Stock Exchange. Madoff had formed a private investment company that seemed to offer good returns on investments that far exceeded the conservative investing Dr. Luddite arranged on behalf of the Foundation. Despite occasional nagging telephone calls from the treasurer, Dr. Luddite continued to place the Foundation's investments in less risky, and less lucrative, investments. When the Madoff scandal broke in 2008, the board recognized that had Dr. Luddite followed its directive, the Foundation's assets would have been completely wiped out.

In almost every case when he had ignored the direction of the board, Dr. Luddite's instincts were prescient, and it was rare that anyone on the board ever pointed out his occasional lapses of blatant insubordination. In almost every case, a reasonable person would have concluded in retrospect that it would have been disastrous for some of the board's direction to have been followed. For years, board chairs had given Dr. Luddite some slack to use his judgment, even if he might have to violate a board resolution in spirit, if not the letter.

Clearly, his experience and his commitment to the welfare of the families the organization served were evident, and his paramount concern during his tenure as the CEO was never himself. The board was grateful that he had been willing to accept a 10% pay cut during last year's budget shortfall, and the organization's revenues were enhanced by book royalties from a primer on Asperger's Syndrome he had authored and that he had designated to be paid to the organization rather than to himself.

Board members and chairs came and went. Dr. Luddite was the public face and voice of the organization, and most would concede that even with his limitations, replacing Dr. Luddite when he chose to retire would be traumatic for the organization and the cause it advanced.

Yet, at least three members of the board were actively seeking to have Dr. Luddite removed from his position and were clamoring for his head on a platter. And they were finding increasing support from a cadre of relatively newly-elected board members who were sympathetic to a change in direction for the organization and were jockeying for either a change in staff leadership or a change in marching orders provided to the current leadership. These two factions of board members were in an alliance against the executive director, but it was clear to Mr. Huddleston that if they succeeded, they would be in opposition to themselves if and when the axe fell on Dr. Luddite. And if they succeeded, the continued viability of the organization might well be threatened, as several major funders remained under the spell Dr. Luddite was able to cast on them and provided grants on the basis of Dr. Luddite's star power. If Dr. Luddite went down, the generous funding from these donors would likely be history. And Mr. Huddleston was in the middle of it all.

For his part, despite imploring from Mr. Huddleston, Dr. Luddite refused to help his own case, which Huddleston attributed to simple stubborn arrogance. He ran the organization virtually the same way he had when he first established the organization. The good news was that he ran the organization with energy and vigor, bristling with integrity that was communicated to the Foundation's ten employees through both deed and word. Even now, approaching 75, he could be seen bounding up three flights of steps to the organization's offices rather than taking the elevator. Although health might become an issue in future years, none of his detractors on the board dared to make the case that he no longer had the mental or physical capacity to lead the organization. Rather, the problem, admittedly becoming a more serious problem with the passage of time, was that Dr. Luddite was technophobic.

This had been amusing at times during the 1980s, as the business world had embraced the productivity increases spurred on by the personal computer. Dr. Luddite would still be seen at his state office into the late hours hunching over at his desk banging out letters and reports on the trusty old Remington typewriter he had used to type his doctoral dissertation in the late '60s. During the 1990s, this was becoming less amusing to observers and more inconvenient. And entering the 21st century, some members of the board recognized that this was becoming a real problem that needed to be addressed. The world had changed almost overnight.

Nonprofit organizations were clearly always several years behind their for-profit counterparts in adopting new technology. But at some point, every nonprofit organization came to understand the role technology had in improving the way they delivered goods and services, and in communicating with their stakeholders. And, more and more, stakeholders of nonprofits had come to expect the organizations to use these new technologies.

Dr. Luddite spurned offers of training, and Huddleston's predecessor as chair once had given an ultimatum that Dr. Luddite needed to learn some new skills or face some sanctions. But that chair had rotated off the board to an amorphous "advisory committee" before achieving any change in the executive director's behavior. The situation today was different; the board's new policy to evaluate the executive director provided an ill-timed forum to discuss Dr. Luddite's glaring weaknesses, which in previous years were simply ignored.

Looking around the room, Mr. Huddleston estimated that at least 14 of the 16 board members present had used either their cell phones or Blackberries to check their e-mail during the meeting. Perhaps half of them had sent a text message— Mr. Huddleston had received three of these messages himself within just the last 30 minutes. The last one was from one board member sitting not more than three feet away across the table, John Winters, a balding, corpulent man in his mid-50s who didn't need to take the entire 140-character limit of the Twitter.com application.

"Time 2 fir tht old dinasr," read the message.

Mr. Huddleston shuddered to think who else in the room had received the same direct message from Winters. But one thing was for certain; it wouldn't have been Dr. Luddite, who refused to even carry a cell phone.

The organization had a working Web site, but it was something that Dr. Luddite had managed, totally by outsourcing, simply to assuage the board. He did not participate in making the site interactive, such as by posting a blog, or by providing electronic newsletters. While his colleagues in the nonprofit community were using the Internet to recruit employees and volunteers, raise funds through online charitable auctions, fundraise and friendraise using Facebook and MySpace pages, and forge revenue-generating affiliation agreements with online retailers, Dr. Luddite turned up his nose at almost any suggestion that related to harnessing the power of the Internet. He refused to even have an e-mail address and would not have had any idea how to access any e-mail he received had he had one. He was a master at one-on-one meetings and radiated a personal charisma that won over many a person who might have been oppositional.

But today, Dr. Luddite was besieged by a phalanx of board members intent to can him and, perhaps, replace him with a younger person who had not even been born when personal computers had been invented.

Despite this disdain for technology, Huddleston was a strong supporter of Dr. Luddite, but recognized that this aspect of his personality could well be the Achilles Heel that resulted in his dismissal, if not at this meeting, at a future one. And the seeds of a potential firing had been sown two years earlier when the board, under the urging of a new organization funder, agreed to institute an annual evaluation of the executive director. At the time, no one was questioning Dr. Luddite's leadership of the organization, and this was considered to be a *pro forma* initiative. Most thought it made sense anyway, as eventually, the reins of leadership would change. Whoever led the organization should be subject to a periodic board evaluation, certainly one of the management controls that are expected to be under the purview of the board. Unfortunately, the addition of three new board members, each of them sporting the latest model of iPhone that appeared to be in constant use, were feeding calls for the board to fire Dr. Luddite.

Mr. Huddleton suspected that in front of him, there was a meeting within a meeting, as the three primary conspirators plotted to fire the executive director, texting among themselves, exchanging strategy.

Joining these three insurgents were several board members who felt that the mission of the organization was too narrowly focused, and that the concentration on Asperger's should be broadened to include all Autism Spectrum Disorders (ASD). They did not feel that Dr. Luddite was willing to extend the reach of the services provided by the organization to serve the growing number of families with a family member having an ASD diagnosis. And perhaps two other board members felt that Dr. Luddite was getting too old and should retire, and that the board should hire someone who would provide fresh leadership. Each had felt some sense of being betrayed by Dr. Luddite whenever he had ignored a board resolution.

Mr. Huddleston estimated that if anyone made a motion to remove Dr. Luddite, perhaps eight of the 16 in the room would join together to force him out, despite having disparate reasons for doing so. The board consisted of 21 members, and five of them were absent. All five were long-time board members, and would likely support Dr. Luddite if they were present. He considered whether to invite them to participate in the meeting by conference call for a reconsideration of the vote if the motion to fire received a majority, but he hoped to avoid a showdown.

Discussion Questions:

1. Is it ever appropriate for an executive director to ignore the express directive of the board or chair of the board?

2. When is it appropriate for a board chair to take actions to remove members of the board for other than missing board meetings or not participating in working on behalf of the organization?

3. Was it appropriate for Dr. Luddite's wife to serve on the board at the time he was the executive director?

4. How much loyalty does a nonprofit organization owe to a long-time executive director whom it judges, for reasons beyond that staff member's control, to be underperforming?

5. How much additional power does the chair of the board typically have compared to any other member of the board? Discuss how this power can be abused.

6. What are ways members of the board can deal with a chair who has Founders Syndrome?

7. What does it mean that "It was Dr. Luddite's job to manage and the board's job to govern"? What are the differences between these two tasks?

Case 7

Navigating a Dual Relationship at the Public Interest Policy Center

With only a single item on the agenda and to the consternation of the chair, the board meeting was starting to deteriorate into a free-for-all of shouting, recriminations, accusations, and name calling.

Denise Willow, the besieged executive director of the Public Interest Policy Center, was the general target of the verbal arrows slung by individual board members who felt betrayed upon learning even more salacious details of Denise's behavior relating to the William A. Ivystone Foundation, the Center's newest and at the moment, largest funder. She did have some defenders among her board, mostly among the handful of female members who were more sympathetic about Denise's assertion that there was a de facto double standard that applied to men and women in her position.

Certainly, no one on the board had ever complained when Denise had used her charm and more than ample physical attractiveness to schmooze up potential donors and entice them into supporting the Center. However, there had to be some reasonable limits to how far a staff member could appropriately play that game without risking serious damage to the Center's respected reputation. It was clear to everyone in the room, including Denise, that someone needed to put on the brakes on this runaway train—thus the call by the chair of the board of the Center for this emergency board meeting to decide what steps to take. None of the apparent options was attractive. *We are in damage control mode here,* thought David Payton, Esq., the chair.

The meeting was in its third hour of contentious wrangling. Denise had been granted all the time she asked for to relate her side of the story, providing even more details about her relationship with William Ivystone, the Foundation President, than some board members present felt were necessary. She explained to the board that she recognized the seriousness of the situation, and the board deserved to know what

had happened, as she sat next to the chair at the long, polished oak table in the conference room of Payton & Payton,
P.C.

Several board members had calmly asserted that Denise
clearly had crossed the line of what was acceptable and should
be fired. Others had done so without being calm. And some
other board members were willing to overlook this major in-
discretion, recognizing that Denise had otherwise been a model
manager and leader, and she had acknowledged her failures
in dealing with this situation, showed remorse, and was willing to make things right and move on with that potentially
Herculean task.

Her recent travails accommodating this particular major
donor had begun innocently, and then had incrementally
snowballed into a surreal soap opera that threatened the integrity of the Center and perhaps its continued existence as
an independent public policy think tank. Some on the board,
despite conceding that she had committed a major *faux pas,*
felt uncomfortable firing the Harvard Law School graduate,
and both the first African American and first woman executive director in the Center's seventy-year history.

Denise's hiring had been no accident, coming within a
few months after the local daily newspaper had concluded a
five-part investigation into the diversity, or lack thereof, of
some of the most prominent nonprofit organizations in the
area. The lack of diversity of the Public Interest Policy Center
was particularly egregious, considering its mission to advocate on behalf of the disenfranchised and victims of discrimination, including women and minorities.

Almost the entire board of the Center had consisted of
white males. The Center's professional staff of four had consisted entirely of white males, and the low-salaried support
staff were virtually all female. Everyone affiliated with the organization was embarrassed by the disclosures, particularly
since the Center made a major focus of its efforts addressing
public policy issues relating to the poor, the sick, women,
and minorities. The word "hypocritical" had been used in the
newspaper editorial following up on its investigative exposé.
The state's wire services had picked up the story and dis-
seminated it to the rest of the state.

Spurred to act quickly by some key stakeholders outside of the organization, the board had made a major effort to recruit qualified minority candidates for the executive director's position. That position had become open after the Center's long-time executive director had been recruited as an Assistant Secretary in the Department of Health and Human Services by the Obama Administration. The board had also recognized that it needed itself to become more diverse, and had recruited three new board members—a white female, an Hispanic male, and an African-American female.

Well, that diversity goal certainly wasn't achieved in full just yet, Denise thought wryly, looking at the group around the table that was serving as the inquisition. Of the 16 present, 12 were white males, three were white women, and one was the African-American female. The average age of the board members was perhaps 65, more than twice Denise's age.

Denise felt that those judging her now around the room were unable to empathize with the situation in which she had found herself. She conceded that she had chiefly herself to blame for these circumstances. But she felt that she was the scapegoat for the shortcomings of the board. After all, it was the board that had failed to follow the very parts of the organization's strategic plan to stop the hemorrhage of unnecessary expenditures. That plan, with substantial input from Denise, had proposed creative ways to increase the income of the respected state-based public policy think tank so it would not have to rely on the continued largesse of any single source of funding.

The timing of her current troubled relationship with the board couldn't have been worse. The Ivystone Foundation had appeared out of nowhere almost exactly one year ago. Its President, a knight in shining armor, had offered his substantial resources to the fair maiden to keep the Center afloat during trying economic times. She had certainly done nothing illegal. In her mind, she was the *victim* of this sordid situation, and it was quite possible that she would suffer the consequences of being victimized while the perpetrator would not only escape with impunity but be able to continue as a stalker and sexual predator until someone took a public stand. Not likely that her spineless board of mostly old white men would do any such thing, she judged, as it had a lot to lose.

"Did you sleep with Ivystone?" Manfred Wishnick asked, more of an interrogation than a question, his penetrating icy stare indicating to Denise that he wouldn't believe her answer no matter how she answered. He was a 70-ish board member, the chair of the Resources Committee, who she suspected would not hesitate to offer a motion to summarily fire her if she had nodded her head affirmatively. Mr. Wishnick had been livid when learning that Denise had applied for a grant from the Foundation without first consulting the board. He had been adamant that the board of directors should be consulted about all potential major grants as part of its governance responsibilities, and that the executive director did not have carte blanche authority to submit grant proposals to funders without prior approval by the Resources Committee. The checks and balances inherent in board review were necessary, he asserted, to assure that the terms of the grant didn't violate any board policy, and that any project funded by the grant was consistent with the organization's mission and values. Not everyone on the board, however, shared that view.

"That question is out of order," ruled David Payton, the chair of the board, who had had a good relationship with Denise, at least up until it had leaked out several months ago that there was something going on between her and the Ivystone Foundation President that was more than a professional relationship. Since that time, Denise perceived a more frosty relationship from him that at times bordered on hostility. She knew that if she totally lost his support, she and the Center would part, perhaps today. If it did come to that, it might be difficult to even get a good recommendation to use for her job hunting, let alone the severance pay she would need to pay the bills in the interim. She also knew that if she were fired for misconduct, she would not be eligible for unemployment compensation.

"I think it is quite relevant to our discussion," responded Wishnick, heatedly. "If she is sleeping with a funder, that is a major conflict of interest and colors how she deals with the demands this funder is placing on our organization."

"No, I'm not sleeping with him, and did not sleep with him," she answered truthfully, without waiting for her chair to respond to Wishnick. But it was quite true that they had engaged in almost every kind of inappropriate behavior short of that threshold during the first six months she and the President of the William A. Ivystone Foundation had known each other, and she certainly wasn't planning on sharing any of the sordid details. What had begun as "harmless" flirting had slowly escalated into something more until it had reached a threshold that had made Denise not only uncomfortable but fearful about her personal security. Ivystone had turned into a stalker, once Denise had made it clear that any personal relationship they had was over.

As the board continued its venomous debate, Denise reflected back on how she got here.

When she had first met Ivystone at a public policy conference, sitting next to him quite by accident (or so she thought at the time), she had found him quite attractive and engaging. He was wearing an obviously expensive, custom-tailored suit with an ostentatiously large diamond encrusted wedding band. He had a warm smile and a laugh that had captivated her. She found him, at least initially, to be charming. Denise found the attention he was giving her to be flattering, and they had had a stimulating, spirited conversation about the luncheon speaker's views on "The Future of the Nonprofit Sector."

He had also been a good listener.

Denise had shared with him her frustration with the financial distress of the Center caused by the withdrawal of support of two key individual funders and the decline of individual memberships brought on by the worsening economy. He had been sympathetic, and mentioned that he might be able to help in some way. They had exchanged business cards. She hadn't known at the time that he was the scion and sole heir of a steel industry magnate who had entrusted his son with managing the philanthropic trust fund the elder Ivystone had established more than 30 years previously, now with assets approaching $160 million. He hadn't mentioned at the time that he was affiliated with any foundation. His card simply had his name and a home telephone number. When she got home, she had Googled him and found immediately that he was the President of a major family foundation. This fact had piqued her interest in following up with him soon for one purpose or another. For a fleeting moment, she imagined herself as Mrs. Ivystone, living a lavish lifestyle of summer homes in the Hamptons, the Caribbean, and London, eating at the best restaurants, flying into New York on a private jet simply to see the latest Broadway Show, and perhaps controlling millions of dollars to dole out to various philanthropic causes. That fantasy didn't last very long once Denise recognized that Ivystone had very little else going for him other than good looks, money to burn, and charm. And one obvious complication—he was married to a socialite from another prominent family. Her Google search had also yielded a substantial trove of less flattering hard information as well as gossip, including media accounts of convictions for illegal drug possession and a statutory rape charge that had been dropped after the victim had refused to testify.

Denise had called him first. Over lunch, at a secluded table in a fancy French restaurant, he had offered to provide the Center with Foundation funds. There was no hint of any *quid pro quo* beyond commissioning the Center to simply expand its mission of developing public policy papers.

The initial $5,000 contract he had offered required the Center to provide the Foundation with ten White Papers on public policy issues, along with a political analysis. The issues were clearly within the range of interests of the Center, which might have welcomed doing the papers without any compensation at all had they come from a board member, staff member, or member of the State Legislature. Denise considered this grant to be a windfall, and the Center certainly needed the money. She did not consult with the board before signing the contract.

But then, the relationship with Ivystone started to change into a *Fatal Attraction*-like nightmare involving the intertwining of two individuals and two organizations with polar opposite agendas.

Denise had had no warning that the first, subtle requests to compromise the Center's integrity would escalate into demands that would place the organization in turmoil and threaten its existence. A combination of a poor economy and the loss of several funders had eroded Center revenues. Without his Foundation's money, Denise realized that the Center would be in danger of not making payroll for the first time in its history. Several other policy think tanks in the state capital, both liberal and conservative, had recently folded, victim of some of the factors that were threatening the fiscal health of the Center.

During those first six months after the initial contract, she had negotiated a new series of contracts with the Foundation to prepare various policy papers. Each contract was for a higher amount of funding, certainly welcome to the Center, which was starved for revenues. Yet with each new contract, more lucrative than the one before, the deliverables were policy papers with a focus farther away from the Center's interests of generating public policy recommendations geared to protecting the interests of those with little voice in the State Capitol. What Ivystone was asking for at first, and later demanding to a greater extent, was material that could advance the Ivystone Steel business interests, often directly in conflict with the interests of the disenfranchised the Center was committed to serve, pursuant to its charter and mission statement.

Ivystone's insatiable demands on the organization had escalated with each contract. He had first requested, then demanded, that drafts of each policy paper be submitted to him for review. Denise had complied because of what she felt was a blossoming personal friendship. At first, these drafts came back with only minimal editing. More recently, they had been returned with substantive edits that conflicted with the supporting data and the Center's ideological slant. Denise had felt violated.

Several times, Ivystone had "suggested" that Denise consider hiring various Ivystone cousins for clerical positions. Considering that the Foundation was providing substantial funding, she had complied. At the time, it had seemed a good idea, and she saw it as a way to justify the continued increases in financial support of the Foundation. Now she regretted surrendering to this infiltration of her organization with sycophants without any real talent or motivation to advance the mission of the Center, and who were clearly more loyal to her organization's benefactor than to her and the Center.

Denise also had shepherded through board approval Ivystone's suggestion that the Center honor Senator John Wingnut, a.k.a. "Senator Steel," as its Legislator of the Year, the first Republican state legislator to be so honored in the 20 years the Center had bestowed such an award. During his entire 30-year Senate career, Sen. Wingnut had voted against almost every position advocated by the Center. However, Wingnut was a staunch opponent of the death penalty, not because it was administered unfairly and disproportionately carried out against those who couldn't afford decent legal representation (as the Center had pointed out in various policy papers over the years), but rather because it simply cost the state too much in legal fees to carry out an execution from its initial court decision through all of the appeals process. Denise had rationalized to her board that having Senator Wingnut as a friend of the Center might pay some dividends down the road. Comments from some board members such as "you sleep with dogs you wake up with fleas" still echoed in her head, and more than a few dues-paying Center members had protested the award by refusing to renew their $35 memberships. The grants from Ivystone dwarfed the loss of a few thousand dollars in membership fees. However, Denise mourned the loss of these loyal supporters whose trust had been violated and who were now actively disparaging her organization.

So far, the board had deflected by postponements Ivystone's request to add three of his nominees to the Center's board by explaining the objectives to increase board diversity. Ivystone had accepted the delay in responding to that request, but he was clearly miffed by the constant rebuff of his effort to expand his influence over the Center's governance.

However, his persistent and relentless efforts to slowly invade and conquer the Center were the least of Ivystone's actions that caused Denise substantial personal grief.

Once Denise discovered his past indiscretions—at least those that were transparent through a routine Internet search, she did not find him to be as attractive as she had during their initial times together. She was becoming more adroit at deflecting his almost constant invitations to be alone with him, but felt the relentless pressure. When he called her at home in the evenings, which was often, she always found an excuse to politely terminate the conversation as soon as she could. She briefly considered calling the police when she found him following her one day. But she did not want to alienate him totally, as the contracts to the Center were a lifeline to get it across the bridge to healthier financial times. He had hinted that increasing the annual grants provided by the Foundation from $200,000 to $500,000 would not be unreasonable if the Center's work continued to please him.

Denise had engaged in an elaborate kabuki dance of resistance to the Foundation President's advances. He was constantly plying her with elaborate and expensive gifts, accompanied by incessant entreaties to fly away with him on his private plane to "discuss the Center's future grants." His real intentions were transparent. The only thing that held her back was a feeling of discomfort with getting involved with someone who could hold so much sway over her professional life. And, of course, putting aside the fact that he was married, there were rumors about him that his intentions with respect to those of the opposite sex were, to use a euphemism, less than honorable. When she had recently found evidence that other female staff members of organizations receiving grants from the Foundation were also receiving the same level of attention from its President, she had abruptly stopped seeing him for any reason and informed her board chair about the situation.

As she sat through this board meeting, Denise felt like her head was in a vise. More accurately, it was her organization that was being squeezed. At the time she participated with her board chair in hammering out a formal memorandum of understanding with the Foundation to provide $200,000 annually in funding in exchange for preparing a new series of public policy white papers, the arrangement had sounded almost too good to be true. Now Denise regretted the day she had even heard of the Foundation or its President, who had been making both her personal and professional life miserable.

William A. Ivystone, IV, a. k. a. "Four," as the Foundation's President was called behind his back by his friends and enemies alike (and certainly he had less flattering names ascribed to him by his enemies), acted as if he was royalty, and everyone else, particularly the beneficiaries of the Foundation's millions of grant dollars, was a peon. Those who weren't deemed to be loyal subjects were banished from his Kingdom. Although the chief staff person for the Foundation, he also completely controlled his board of directors, mostly thirty-something blood relatives of William Ivystone, without having a vote himself, or any need to have one.

Those few in the Ivystone clan who had shown any real acumen or talent for business were funneled up the corporate ladder running businesses spun off by the senior Ivystone. The underachievers and slackers, and there were many, were relegated to serving on the philanthropic board, with their modest salary supplemented by the proceeds from the trust fund the elder Ivystone had established for each of his young nieces, nephews, and cousins at birth.

Four had consolidated his power by finding a way to remove those on the board who wouldn't give him a free rein to both manage and govern the Foundation. He ran into little resistance from the board, many of whom were grateful for the $25,000 annual salaries they received for doing absolutely no tasks other than attending the four board meetings each year and perfunctorily voting in favor of making the grants on the list provided to them by their King, William the 4th. Achieving a quorum at these meetings was never in doubt. The saturnalia that followed each board meeting, held in a private suite at the Ritz Carlton, made it worthy to show up. No one on the board cared to inquire whether the cocaine that was available at these parties came from the Foundation's substantial entertainment budget or from the monthly payments from Four's personal trust fund.

It has been said many times that power corrupts and absolute power corrupts absolutely. In all Foundation matters, Four held absolute power and wielded it with impunity. He was a legend for using the resources of the Foundation to advance not only his professional, but also his personal agenda. He acted as if the money doled out by the Foundation was his own, a criticism often leveled at even the most reputable and professional foundation CEOs. He was also alleged to consider female individuals within the organizations benefiting from the Foundation's largesse to be members of his personal harem. It was understood that payments had been made by the Foundation to maintain the silence of several staff members of grantee organizations and others with respect to Four's often inappropriate behavior.

It was also well known throughout the foundation community that Four adroitly steered Foundation grants to his personal friends, and to those with whom he either had personal relationships or to those he desired to pursue for such a purpose.

The day in and day out demands of the Foundation on not only her time but on the soul of the Center had affected Denise not only emotionally, but physically, as well. At her latest meeting with Four, she had felt breathing problems severe enough that an ambulance had to be called. Although a heart attack had not been diagnosed, the cardiologist had found enough abnormalities to admit her for observation. Her blood pressure was high, and the symptoms, which were attributable to a panic attack, had made her realize that she couldn't continue with this relationship, personal or professional.

But cutting the cord and ending the relationship was not quite so simple. Ivystone could, with one stroke of the pen, threaten to end her means of livelihood, as well as the good work the Center did for the poor, needy, ill, aged, and others who had minimal voice on public policy issues at the state level.

Finding a comparable job was out of the question, with unemployment at its highest level in more than a quarter century and growing every day.

She had made the decision to beg and grovel at this board meeting to keep her job, and agree to do whatever it took to return to the time when she had never heard of William Ivystone or his Foundation, even if she had to take a substantial pay cut.

The board continued its bickering, and Denise thought back to things she had learned about the foundation sector in general and the Ivystone Foundation in particular during her ordeal.

The abuses Denise saw within the Ivystone Foundation were far from being an anomaly. Of course, most of the thousands of private foundations authorized under Section 509 of the Internal Revenue Code followed the rules. But there were constant calls for reforming those rules, which many observers, including those within the foundations themselves, conceded did not serve the public interest.

For example, the IRS requires foundations to give out a minimal amount in grants in order to maintain their tax-exempt status, currently just 5% of their net investment returns, a scandalously low amount. What is not generally understood is that these foundations are permitted to include all administrative and operating costs, which may include salaries and fees paid to the foundations' trustees, within that threshold. So in practice, many foundations are able to shelter enormous wealth from taxes, with only minimal amounts of that wealth being allocated for charitable purposes. There are few effective oversight mechanisms to assure that the philanthropy that is intended to benefit the public is not diverted to the personal benefit of those who serve on the foundation boards.

But as Denise came to understand firsthand, being the object of Ivystone's attention was not his only objective. It was not inconceivable that his intention was to convert the Center into a de facto wholly-owned subsidiary of the steel industry's propaganda machine, and thus show to his father that he was capable of taking over the entire family business when the time came for Dad to retire.

Denise, with some relief, heard indications that the meeting was reaching a conclusion and her ordeal would soon be over.

"Well, we have some options here, but none of them are attractive," summarized the board chair. "First, we can cut our losses, do the honorable thing, and sever all contact we have with the Foundation. Going with this option will obviously be traumatic and painfully expensive. We would all have to work together to find a new source of funding to replace this loss of income. We will have to have a major restructuring of our staff to accommodate the cuts to balance a budget." He looked around the room, and half of those present were nodding their heads, and the other half were showing signs of distress about this option.

"A second option might be to salvage the relationship with the Foundation for future contributions by making it clear that the Center must maintain its independence and intellectual integrity, but make sure, by board resolution, that Denise is to have no further direct contact with Mr. Ivystone."

"Denise?" David Payne recognized the CEO.

"First, let me repeat to the board that I am truly sorry for how this turned out. The lesson we should all learn is to check out our prospective donors and grantees thoroughly. And I will do whatever it takes to make things right again. If the board wants me to resign, I will. But I know I can lead this organization back to where it needs and deserves to be, and I hope to regain your trust by working as hard as I can to get us out of this mess."

"Thank you, Denise. Is there a motion on the floor?"

Discussion Questions:

1. How legitimate is Mr. Wishnick's viewpoint that the board should have authority to review all grant proposals beforehand to assure they are consistent with the organization's mission and values? What are the pros and cons of this policy?

2. Why is it important that nonprofit boards have a diverse membership? What are some of the advantages and disadvantages of having such a board?

3. How much of the blame for this situation is attributable to Denise? What could she have done to avoid the situation she now finds herself in?

4. Should the board fire Denise? If not, what other discipline, if any, would be appropriate? What should the board do to resolve the problems caused by this funder?

5. How much should the fact that Denise is a woman and minority factor into the board's decision concerning this case?

6. Why do public policy makers and the public, as well, accept the status quo with respect to the legal minimum of how much charity foundations are required to do to maintain their tax-exemptions?

Case 8

Gambling on an Outside Fundraising Consultant for the "For the Kids" Shelter

Brittany Lohman, the twenty-something CEO of the "For the Kids" shelter for runaway teenagers, was getting angry at the intransigence of her board in refusing to approve her new fundraising proposal. She tried not to display her irritation. They kept raising questions, some of which made her uncomfortable. Some of these questions were good ones that she couldn't answer. At best, she thought that the board would delay making a final decision on the proposal, which might make it too late to take advantage of what she saw as a great opportunity.

To Brittany, this should have been a "no brainer" for her board. After all, she felt certain there was absolutely nothing for the organization to lose from signing a contract with Bennett Fundraising Associates (BFA), a for-profit professional fundraising consulting and management company. At worst, the shelter would get a promised upfront payment of $400 from the arrangement, even if Vinny Bennett's plans for generating thousands of dollars in new donations for the shelter ended up a total disaster, and the likelihood of that outcome was negligible. No shelter funds would be required either as startup capital or if the arrangement resulted in any financial loss—the contract language Mr. Bennett provided to Brittany clearly stipulated that Bennett Fundraising Associates would do all of the advance work, assume all the risk, and finance all upfront costs. What downside could possibly convince her board to disapprove of this?!

Well, now after more than an hour of contentious debate, she had a better idea of some of the downsides that she admitted she had failed to consider. Still, it made sense to just do it. The proposed contract ran for only a year, and if it didn't work out, the shelter had the option simply to not renew it.

She vividly remembered the part of the pitch Bennett had made that had sold her on the concept.

"There is only one task we won't do for you," Bennett had shared with a conspiratorial smile. "You have to deposit the check we send you into your bank account. Anything else that is needed, we will do." That had been an effective close. Now, she wished he was in the room to deal with her recalcitrant board members. He would not only have glib responses, but get a sense of what she was dealing with in order to get approval for the contract.

Brittany wasn't prepared for the firestorm of opposition from board members who usually had been counted on to approve her proposals perfunctorily. This should not have even been controversial, she thought. Are they being oppositional for reasons having nothing to do with this proposal? There had to be something her board members found objectionable other than the contract. Every disadvantage of doing this was clearly counterbalanced by better reasons to forge ahead, she thought.

As Mr. Bennett himself had told her with confidence, it was not likely that this venture would lose money, and if it did, "For the Kids" would still receive $400. BFA would incur all of the losses, if any. Many other local organizations had received substantial checks from participating in this program, he intimated without naming any, because the names of his other clients, other than a handful who provided testimonials, were "proprietary."

The shelter would receive $400 immediately from BFA as soon as the contract was signed. The check the shelter would receive within two weeks of the completion of the fundraising special event conducted on its behalf required virtually no work by the charity benefitting from the program, and it could potentially amount to thousands of dollars. All the organization had to do was sign the contract, give BFA access to its mailing list of current board members and contributors and those who received its newsletter, sit back, and then cash the checks it would receive. BFA would do all of the work in generating charitable contributions through its latest collaborative program for charities.

It was all perfectly legal, and Mr. Bennett had brandished an advisory opinion from an attorney's office located in the state's largest city, or so Brittany gathered from the stationery, certifying that a charitable organization would not be violating any state or federal gambling laws by participating in this program. Also in the information packet he provided to her were testimonials from staff members of several other local charities that had participated in Mr. Bennett's program. She hadn't recognized the names of any of the organizations, none of which were particularly well-known, but she had looked online at their Web sites, and they had appeared to be legitimate.

Basically, what BFA offered to do was hold a "Texas Hold 'em Tournament for Charity" night at a local volunteer fire hall in Harristown. BFA would send mailings and e-mails to stakeholders of the shelter inviting them to the fundraiser, supplementing that list with its own list of hundreds of "regulars" who would attend these BFA-managed fundraisers, regardless of the beneficiary.

State law expressly prohibited gambling other than the state lottery, administered by the state to benefit education, and pari-mutuel betting on horseracing, heavily regulated with no opportunity for new entrants. But there was a loophole permitting charities with 501(c)(3) tax-exempt status to hold an annual, one-day-only, fundraising event that included gambling if all net proceeds were allocated to the charity. When the Legislature had passed this law, several safeguards were put in place. One such statutory requirement was that the event needed to be staffed and conducted entirely by employees of the charity. Few, if any, charities had the capacity or experience to stage events like this. The "one-time only annually" restriction made it not cost-effective for charities to purchase the equipment needed for these events, and few took advantage of this provision in the law, according to Mr. Bennett.

And that was where BFA came in, he explained.

What BFA offered was a service that involved doing all of the paperwork involved in hiring its own trained staff as employees of its charity clients for a single day, and having those employees reimbursed for the reasonable and actual expenses incurred in putting on the event. BFA would be in the background, orchestrating all of the management tasks, for which it would be paid a reasonable fee out of the proceeds from the fundraiser. The terms of the contract for BFA stipulated that if the event did not raise at least $400 for its charity client above any expenses paid out, that fee would be waived, and the expenses would be reimbursed by a donation made to the charity by BFA. And in the almost certain event that the fundraiser returned net "donations" in excess of this $400, BFA and the charity would split that amount 50-50 after expenses were deducted.

This arrangement was not dissimilar to a method of fundraising that had become very popular in recent years, involving arrangements between charities and local restaurants, Bennett said. Charities and cooperating restaurants would establish an evening during which the restaurant would donate a percentage of its receipts that night to a particular charity. That charity would cooperate in encouraging its supporters to patronize the restaurant on the designated evening. One difference in BFA's model was that the restaurant might at most raise a couple of hundred dollars for the charity. A BFA-managed event could possibly attract a thousand people, many of whom hadn't even heard of the charity. The funds raised typically could range from a thousand dollars to as much as twenty-thousand dollars.

"Imagine what the shelter could do with an extra $20,000," he suggested. "There is, of course, no guarantee that this will be the amount you get out of this, but it wouldn't be unusual, considering that some of our regular players attend with a roll of hundreds the size of your fist."

Mr. Bennett had explained that playing poker was quickly becoming one of America's most popular pastimes, with as many as 100 million adults playing regularly, more than double the number who had participated just a couple of decades earlier. It was quite expensive to travel to places such as Las Vegas or Atlantic City to play in states that had legalized casino gambling. Access to live, legal games had expanded as casinos on Indian reservations in additional states had expanded gambling opportunities.

Although the Internet provided virtual venues that were both legal and illegal, many players simply did not trust these sites, and there was only a minimal fraction of the excitement players felt by gambling in a lively social atmosphere.

Why should all of this money go to the government or for-profit entrepreneurs? Shouldn't charities participate in getting a piece of this action? The State Legislature certainly agreed, as they had provided for this particular law to help charities finance their good works. The only barrier to diverting some of this money to charities was a simple action of asking for some of it. This is what BFA was all about, he had told her. Everyone wins. Even those who lost money gambling had an evening out with some of their money going to a good cause.

These BFA-managed events not only would mean donations to the shelter. Attendees would have the opportunity to learn about the shelter's good work. Mr. Bennett had told Brittany that it was not unusual for the victor of the evening's Texas hold'em jackpot prize to donate his or her entire winnings back to the charity sponsoring the event. And when they did that, the charity received 50% of that donation, a windfall it would never have received otherwise.

There was a group of dedicated recreational poker players who attended the circuit of events managed by BFA, and many of them had lots of disposable income, Bennett had pointed out. Their exposure to charities that were BFA clients came only from their participation in the poker games. When they sent a check directly to the charity, which happened often, ALL of those funds went to the charity.

As an added bonus, BFA would manage and run the concession stands at the event, and "For the Kids" would receive 10% of the net proceeds from that operation, he said.

This was a limited opportunity, as there were only so many open dates to have an event managed by BFA. Once these slots were filled with other charities, there would be no opportunity to add "For the Kids." Unless the organization gave the go-ahead and signed a contract within 30 days, this opportunity would likely be lost.

But as Brittany sat in her board meeting trying to explain the details, she judged quickly that her board was less than impressed by the proposal. This was not the first time she could recall a lucrative opportunity being lost because a for-profit collaborator had been unable or unwilling to commit to a timeframe required for a nonprofit organization to process a binding decision. Many for-profit entrepreneurs became frustrated waiting for a board to approve a decision agreed to tentatively by an executive director, only to have the board delay a final decision until a board committee could make a full report at a subsequent board meeting. And board members, unlike those of a for-profit board, often did not share the same agenda.

Whereas everyone on a for-profit board shared the general goal of making as much profit as possible, there were typically many competing interests within a nonprofit board. The diversity of such a board, often viewed as an asset, also has a cost in that members often do not share the same values. As Brittany made the case for board approval of this contract, she had to concede that there were conflicting values among her board members that threatened what she thought should be routine approval.

She listened as the debate droned on and on.

"What message does this send to the community and to our young clients? Is gambling something we want to send a message to encourage?" asked Pete Hemphill, a real estate agent whom she knew was quite a gambler himself, albeit allegedly addicted to betting on sports events.

Anticipating some of these questions, Brittany had provided the board with a short position paper to justify participation, prepared using a template provided by BFA. In the paper, she noted some of the pros and cons of gambling. For example, for all but a small percentage of individuals, gambling was harmless entertainment. The event would keep dollars locally that might otherwise be diverted to other communities that permitted legalized gambling. It created jobs. It siphoned dollars away from illegal gambling, which would be available if the legal market did not satisfy its customers. And, in this particular case, it could provide an incentive for individuals to donate money that would support a worthy charity such as For the Kids.

On the flip side, there were studies that measured that 1-5% of those who gambled did so compulsively and destructively, and there were economic, psychological, and other costs involved, such as the social ills that accompanied the expansion of access to gambling.

Among these were the costs of policing and dealing with the infusion of organized crime figures who found gambling as an attractive method of generating relatively untraceable cash out of the reach of taxing bodies.

"Lots of charities have a casino night or Monte Carlo night, and I've been to a few of them myself," added Harold Fallwell, III, a used car dealer who owned several lots in the poorer areas of town. "But I've never been to one that had cash prizes, and where those who attend aren't somehow affiliated with the charity. My problem with this is that it appears to me that most of the money generated by this would go to BFA."

"I agree that this is problematic. As I read this contract, For the Kids receives 50% of the 'net revenue' and BFA receives the other half," commented Dorothy Willingham, a board member who also served as a volunteer in the shelter, playing the piano two nights each week to entertain the residents. "As I understand it, the way the contract defines 'net revenue' is revenue after expenses, and the term 'expenses' is defined in the contract in such a way that it covers the costs of personnel running the events, in addition to all of the other costs such as advertising, security, mailing, and hall rental. The way I interpret this contract is that it is possible that the 'fundraiser' for For the Kids, even if it generated let's say $10,000 in 'donations' for the event, we might only get the base four hundred dollars once all of these expenses are taken into account. BFA could pocket thousands from the management fee and using the expenses to cover its overhead."

"Okay, I would concede that, but that's $400 more than we are receiving now, and if we did this every year, we could generate some real dollars without having to do any work or incur any costs or risks," countered Steve Bartholomew, a new board member who worked as a state caseworker in the Department of Families and Youth. "I passed the fire house once when they were having one of these tournaments. I could tell the place was packed, and there were a bunch of police cars outside with their red lights flashing—I guess there was some altercation going on, which made me notice what was going on at the hall."

"Well, that brings up another question then," responded Ellen Simpson, a nurse from Harristown Hospital. "Would the shelter have any liability if something bad happened at this event? After all, the contract provides that everyone running the fundraiser is a shelter employee. I know volunteers have some protection, and nonprofit organizations have limited liability, but we have no idea who these employees would be. Would they have the same State Police background checks required of our own employees?"

"And another issue concerns me," chimed in Marilyn Able, a major contributor to the shelter who had been a charter member of the board when it was first formed almost 20 years earlier. "Doesn't anyone have any qualms about us sharing our mailing list with a for-profit provider who is using our organization's good name to earn its living?"

"Good point, Marilyn. I share that concern," responded Tim Hope, the owner of a local beer distributorship. "But even more of a concern to me, do we really want to raise money through gambling? What message does this send to the kids in the shelter, and to those in the community who we want to support us?"

There was general assent that this was an important issue. But Brittany refused to give up.

"This wouldn't be my first choice of fundraising efforts," Brittany responded. "If the board had approved the proposal I made at the last meeting, we would have invested $20,000 in hiring a part-time, in-house fundraiser who would find a way to generate enough funds to pay their salary while raising more. Fundraising takes a lot of work and effort. And money. Money we simply don't have. And I don't have the time to plan and execute the activities necessary to raise money while doing all the other things necessary to run the shelter and keep it afloat. I would prefer it if we had enough stable income from grants and donations to keep things going, but as you can figure out from hearing the Treasurer's Report, we are building ourselves a deficit that will be difficult, if not impossible, to overcome unless we do something new.

"Now, here's one way we can get a new source of revenue without any upfront costs—as we would have had if we had hired a staff person to do the fundraising in-house—or any risk. What is the problem with this! We have nothing to lose; the contract makes it clear that we will get a minimum of $400 simply by agreeing to partner with BFA, and the potential is there to get something substantial out of this!"

Rather than soothing the board, members appeared to become even more agitated, and peppered Brittany with even more questions and concerns, coming rapid fire.

I don't see anything in this contract that says the mailing list we provide cannot be used for other purposes than what we authorize, and even if it did have such a clause, how do we know we can trust this company?

Is there a list of clients? How do we know we don't have the stories of those who did not feel that this was such a good deal for them?

Have you talked with any staff of other organizations who have used the services of this company?

What is the background of Mr. Bennett? Has he operated this business in our state or other states without any problems? Who owns the company?

Is he or his company even registered as a professional fundraiser with the Bureau of Charitable Organizations? What more can we find out about him?

Brittany suddenly realized that the board would not likely give the approval she had needed, which she had all but promised Mr. Bennett would be routine. Well, maybe some of the concerns of the board were legitimate.

"Okay, I get the message," Brittany conceded. "Let me get some more information about how this would work and about who we are dealing with. But I ask that the board authorize the executive committee to act on this matter in advance of the next board meeting, as this will no longer be an option by the time the board meets again in three months. I have less than 30 days to get this approved, or the offer will be withdrawn."

"Sounds fair and reasonable, and I so move," responded the chair. "All those in favor of the motion to do this indicate by saying 'Aye,' all opposed "Nay." The motion has carried unanimously.

"Now," continued the chair, "let's move on to the next agenda item about what we need to do to raise the $20,000 we need to balance the current year's budget...."

Discussion Questions:

1. What are some of the "red flags" in this story that might indicate that there is something not quite legitimate with BFA and its fundraising model?

2. What is the role of board and staff in deciding whether to participate in this proposed cooperative venture?

3. What are some of the ethical dilemmas involved in having a cooperative agreement with a for-profit company that seeks to exploit charities?

4. How inappropriate is it for this fundraiser to be a gambling event, compared to, for example, a meal at a local restaurant?

5. What might be some of the legal problems involved in this proposal?

6. What might Brittany have done to better research BFA and its President?

7. Discuss the problems that occur when decisions of a nonprofit organization must be made by a committee that may meet only every three months? What decisions should be the purview of the board, and when should staff have the authority to make decisions?

Case 9

Reporting Financial Misconduct at Uncommon Agenda

Jack looked at his computer screen and read the e-mail again. And again. He felt a mix of emotions, among them apprehension, anger, disgust, fear, rage, and astonishment knowing that his life was about to change as a result of reading the content of this electronic message that was intended for his best friend rather than himself. He knew immediately that nothing good would come of this, but that it would be difficult to predict what would happen other than that it would definitely be bad.

Jack was the IT Director for Uncommon Agenda, a nonprofit, 501(c)(4) tax-exempt advocacy organization based in Washington, D.C. with field operations in six states. Nonprofit organizations granted tax exempt status under this provision of the Internal Revenue Code are designated as "social welfare" organizations rather than charities. Although 501(c)(3) organizations are permitted by law to lobby, they are prohibited by law from doing so in a "substantial" amount. In contrast, social welfare organizations are permitted to lobby to the extent they desire, and most of these organizations are formed for the primary purpose of lobbying and advocacy.

One major disadvantage of exemption under 501(c)(4), however, is that those who contribute to these organizations are not eligible to deduct contributions to them on their federal income tax returns. However, many such organizations have affiliated 501(c)(3)s that accept tax deductible contributions and then transfer those donations to fund the operations of the (c)(4). Unlike their charitable counterparts, social welfare organizations may engage in partisan political activities and support candidates for office, although there is a substantial excise tax associated with such expenditures. Many 501(c)(4) organizations, such as Uncommon Agenda, do not engage in overt partisan activity, and boast that their good government activities are nonpartisan.

The mission of Uncommon Agenda was to build support for public funding of Congressional campaigns. It worked in coalition with like-minded organizations to advocate for such funding. Although the organization solicited memberships from the public at $25 annually, most of its funding came from several large foundations that shared the vision of the organization to end the rampant abuses of campaign financing by lobbyists and others with a direct interest in legislative decision-making. Critics charged that special interests skewed public policy toward the privileged, and that the current system of campaign finance ultimately cost the public billions of dollars in wasteful spending of tax dollars and tax expenditures.

Uncommon Agenda was located in a slightly run-down office building on Connecticut Avenue in Northwest Washington, near the zoo. On most business days, the office was a beehive of activity, the phones ringing, meetings being held to plot strategy, fundraising plans being developed, and 20-something staff members who had only recently served as college interns on the Hill contacting Congressional staff to seek support for the latest version of a bipartisan public campaign financing bill.

Oblivious to most of the activity were a couple of support staff who were not directly engaged in the quest to achieve reform of campaign finance laws. One of these was Jack, the IT Director, who had a nondescript office far away from the main entrance. There was no window; his office was in an inside corridor, deep in the bowels of the 7th floor. Jack's office was lined mostly with software rather than books. Stacked high in a corner was a pile of boxes that held an assortment of equipment one might expect to find in the office of the IT head—assorted mice, cables, wireless modems, old keyboards, laptops that were in various stages of disrepair, and tools.

On most days, Jack was not particularly busy. He may have had some staff training to demonstrate to a group of employees how to use the organization's upgraded software, or to orient a new hire about how to use the existing packages that were on the network. He was also responsible for keeping the Web site in working order and sending out bulk electronic newsletters and fundraising e-mail. On occasion, things got really busy. When that happened, such as when the system server went down or if there was a Denial of Service attack on the Web site, he was expected to work through the night when necessary to get things back in order.

But nothing in his five years in this position prepared him for the situation he found himself in today.

It was mid-March, and Washington was experiencing unseasonably hot weather, coaxing the cherry blossoms to bloom a few days earlier than the official start of the Cherry Blossom Festival still two weekends away. In mid-February, a man's heart might turn to thoughts of love. But in mid-March, it turns to college basketball. Even the President interrupted dealing with an economy that was tanking and crises around the planet to fill out his NCAA brackets along with millions of others.

On Friday afternoon, Jack had received a call on the office intercom system from Steve Pearson, the Vice President for Operations, about a problem he was having accessing his e-mail. Steve was a congenial colleague, as well as a personal friend from Jack's grad school days. It was not unusual for Steve to join him and one other colleague, Bill Higgins, who was V.P. for Human Resources at Uncommon Agenda, to hang out together on Friday nights. They usually frequented a couple of clubs in Georgetown and got drunk together. Lately, Steve had been paying the entire tab for the three of them, explaining that he had just come into a windfall when a childless, distant aunt had died and left her nephews some money.

All of them had come to the organization at about the same time, when it was first formed with a seven-figure combined grant from three national private foundations. Steve had joined the staff first and had suggested that Jack consider leaving his job in New York to fill an opening for IT Director.

Jack was not particularly interested in the nonprofit sector in general, or the organization in particular, when he applied for that position. He would have been just as happy working for IBM or Microsoft. What attracted him were the downtown Washington, D.C. location and the likelihood that he would have a comfortable salary and not have the pressure of working in a typical corporate environment. He had interviewed elsewhere, but was attracted to the casual working atmosphere and the likely prospect that he would be in charge of the department. Actually, he would be the only member of the department, without the annoyance of having to supervise others and with no one looking over his shoulder all of the time. The people he saw in the office seemed quite happy with their jobs and were devoted to the organization's mission. This was certainly in contrast to where he had been working at the time, which he referred to as a software sweatshop where he was required to meet a quota of several thousand lines of code each week.

When Steve, one of his roommates while he was a graduate student getting his MBA from Columbia, told him about the position opening up at Uncommon Agenda, Jack had been flattered and had been delighted to consider leaving the Big Apple. He and Steve were buddies, and Steve had covered for him many times with a girlfriend who was insanely jealous of Jack seeing other women during his relationship with her. Steve had been counted on by Jack to tell more than a lie or two to preserve the relationship, and Steve never let him down. Without Steve around at Uncommon Agenda, Jack might well have left for something else.

It had only been minutes earlier that Jack felt that his life was being turned upside down. It had all started when he had heard a buzzer in the office indicating that he was being called on the intercom system. It was Steve. He expected Steve to review the plans they had for cruising Georgetown the following evening in Steve's new BMW, but instead, it was to relay a problem Steve was having with accessing his e-mail.

"I haven't received any e-mail for four hours now, and I know something is wrong," Steve told him. Almost all of the communications between them during office hours were by e-mail, but without access to that mode of communication, Steve resorted to the more primitive intercom system.

"Let me check it out," Jack had said, planning to see if anyone else in the office was also having this problem. Jack himself hadn't noticed any problem accessing his work e-mail, although such e-mails were infrequent except when there was an IT problem. He, like most staff of Uncommon Agenda, kept a separate e-mail account for his personal mail. There was a written policy that every staff member was entitled to an organization e-mail account, and the organization would respect the privacy of e-mail sent and received on work computers. The few restrictions on this use were that the organization's computers could not be used for illegal purposes, to access pornography, or to violate copyright laws. Jack had thought this policy was flawed, since how would he or anyone in the organization determine if anyone was using the office computers inappropriately without first violating the privacy explicitly provided by the policy? In five years as IT Director, this issue had never surfaced.

Jack always encouraged new staff members to avoid using Uncommon Agenda e-mail accounts for their personal e-mail, and only a handful of staff members did not have separate accounts for their personal e-mail. This was not only recommended to maintain privacy, but to save on bandwidth. With the capacity to download not only music clips but even full-length movies, Jack felt the obligation to conserve organizational resources and not overload the capacity of the server.

Jack was not working on anything in particular when Steve called, but he was still annoyed that he would be diverted from watching some of the action in the first round of the NCAA basketball tournament that was being streamed in real time to his cell phone. A number 15 seed was hanging tough against a number two. Ah, the benefits of technology, Jack thought.

From his office, Jack had begun troubleshooting this new glitch, and came across nearly a score of e-mails that were caught in the network's spam filter that appeared to be potentially legitimate e-mails. Clicking on one of several addressed to Steve, it was clear that this particular e-mail to Steve wasn't spam, with a .ch country code top level domain name that he didn't immediately recognize.

Reading the e-mail, he quickly confirmed his suspicions that it was not spam. What it appeared to be was a confirmation of a bank transfer involving a transaction from the Washington Capital Bank and Trust Company to a bank in Switzerland. Reading it more closely, the transfer appeared to Jack to involve a transfer of $8,000 from an account belonging to Uncommon Agenda to a numbered account. Jack was quite certain that Uncommon Agenda didn't use banks in Switzerland, and that the organization certainly wouldn't use a numbered account. Uncommon Agenda publicly and stridently railed against the lack of transparency of the way cash for political campaigns was funneled into the system. In any case, even if the organization had a legitimate reason for getting involved in having a numbered Swiss account, it would be unlikely that Steve would have had the authority to move funds from the organization to such an account. Clearly, the Chief Financial Officer, Carol Henfield, would be the individual from the organization with authority to move funds in this way. Knowing Carol, it was quite unlikely that she would have anything to do with numbered Swiss accounts, even if the money was her own personal funds. This was not consistent with her personality, which was doing absolutely everything by the book. While liberal in ideology, she was so conservative that he surmised that she never failed to look both ways even when crossing a one-way street.

Jack's policy was to routinely delete the master file of copies of e-mails every month. Curious about this discovery, however, he searched in the database of archived organization e-mails and looked at more e-mails to Steve. For each of the previous four weeks, the number of weeks that old e-mails were still available in the system (other than on the computers of those who received them, unless they were deleted by those individuals), there was a receipt from this bank for $8,000 of funds transferred out of an account in the name of Uncommon Agenda under the total control of Steve, to the numbered account.

Jack was in shock that his long-time friend and colleague appeared to be an embezzler. Could there be some other, innocent, explanation for these transfers? Not likely, but it was possible. Embezzling would explain a few things, such as the new BMW.

But the more pressing concern was what he should do with this information. Steve was his best friend in Washington.

What if there were others in the organization involved in this other than Steve? Would his job be at risk if he reported this to the CEO? He remembered something from a recent staff meeting about Uncommon Agenda being in the process of creating a whistleblower policy. Doing so had been motivated by something that had appeared on the revised 990 annual tax return for tax-exempt nonprofit organizations. This meant that Uncommon Agenda did not currently have such a policy in force. Someone had mentioned at the meeting that there was a federal law on whistleblowing that applied to nonprofits, but that it was quite inadequate to protect anyone except under the most limited of circumstances.

Curious, he Googled "whistleblower" "nonprofit" "federal" and came up with something called the "Sarbanes-Oxley" law enacted in 2002. Yes, that was the name he had heard at the meeting! Finding the full text of the law, he searched on some terms and found the following:

Sec. 1107. RETALIATION AGAINST INFORMANTS.

(a) IN GENERAL- Section 1513 of title 18, United States Code, is amended by adding at the end the following: (e) Whoever knowingly, with the intent to retaliate, takes any action harmful to any person, including interference with the lawful employment or livelihood of any person, for providing to a law enforcement officer any truthful information relating to the commission or possible commission of any Federal offense, shall be fined under this title or imprisoned not more than 10 years, or both.

He interpreted that to mean that if he reported Steve's e-mail to law enforcement authorities, he would have protection to keep his job. But if he reported this to anyone inside the organization, he would be at risk. *You would think that the organization would rather have misconduct reported internally so they can deal with it, or cover it up better,* he thought.

Jack, still shocked that his buddy appeared to be siphoning off funds from their employer at potentially the rate of $400,000 annually, took out a pad of paper and started writing out some of his options.

Among the eight options he considered:

1. Confront Steve. Offer to keep quiet in exchange for a share of the funds.
2. Confront Steve, and simply demand that he stop embezzling, quietly make restitution, or risk being turned in to the authorities.

3. Confront Steve, and convince him to come forward to the organization voluntarily and admit what he was doing, leaving Jack out of this.
4. Take the matter to the organization's CEO and CFO without informing Steve.
5. Take the matter to the law enforcement authorities without informing Steve.
6. Let someone know about this within the organization anonymously.
7. Do nothing.
8. Seek advice from a third party, such as a friend or attorney, before taking any action.

Jack's consideration of how to deal with this quandary was interrupted as he saw Steve stick his head into his office.

"Any progress on getting my e-mail?" Steve asked.

"Not yet," Jack lied. "Anything interesting going on?"

"Well, I might not make it for drinks tonight, or at least until much later. There was a front page *New York Times* article this morning about campaign financing, and I've been getting lots of calls from the press as well as my field office folks."

"I didn't see the *Times* today. What was in it?" Jack asked politely, not sharing that he hadn't read the front page of the *Washington Post* that day, instead focusing on the NCAA pairings on the sports page.

"The article estimated that Obama raised an estimated $300 million for the general election, outspending McCain by about 3-1. This was after he had first pledged to accept public financing, and he eventually reneged on that commitment, becoming the first major party candidate to finance his general election campaign with private contributions. McCain only got $84 million for the general. Anyway, the *Times* story estimated that Obama raised an estimated $750 million during the entire campaign from close to four million contributors. Had he not done so, he might have gotten his butt kicked."

Jack listened, feigning interest, but he couldn't care less about campaign finance, somewhat ironic since that was the *raison d'être* of the organization that employed him. He admitted to himself that he considered the entire issue to be really boring.

But the good news was that he wouldn't have to decide what to do about Steve's "problem" today, and he could simply hang out in his office and watch some of the late first-round tournament games, or just go back to his apartment. And decide what to do.

Discussion Questions:

1. How "private" should personal e-mail be if it is sent and received from a nonprofit organization's account?

2. What are the pluses and minuses of each of the eight options on Jack's list?

3. What are the limitations of federal whistleblower protection for nonprofit organizations? What might be appropriate in an organization's whistleblower policy?

4. What are some of the objectives of having an organization whistleblower policy?

5. If you are the CEO of this organization and Jack comes to you and spills the beans, what would your response be?

6. What is Jack's legal responsibility, if any, to let someone know about this? What is Jack's ethical responsibility?

7. How important is it to nonprofit organizations that their staff be committed to the organization's mission and comfortable with the culture of the nonprofit sector, in light of the fact that nonprofit organizations more than ever employ staff who could work in business just as easily, such as Webmasters, accountants, IT professionals, and marketers?

Case 10

The Disruptive Board Member of the Harristown Vet Center

Oliver Hanson was finally coming to the end of his joke, to the relief of everyone in the room.

...and in the morning after Dad goes to work, the milkman will deliver the milk and have his usual "quickie" with Mom....And then, he'll catch the clap, which is just fine with me! He's the @&%$* who ran over my dog!

There was a nervous laugh, a half-hearted groan, and the 13 others sitting around the board room conference table simply remained silent through their discomfort, staring downward, making no eye contact with either the story-teller or the chair. Other than that, there was no outward reaction to the punch line besides the labored chortling of Hanson, whose already ruddy complexion appeared to deepen even more, if that was possible.

Hanson's jokes were unwelcome at any time—they were usually long, off-color, and it was a stretch to consider any of them even moderately amusing. But coming in the middle of a board meeting, these distractions were doubly inappropriate. Other board members had been complaining about Hanson's incessant interruptions, which often came when the board's deliberations were peaking at the most intense moments. Some found him annoying, while others labeled his behavior insufferable. Without warning, he would launch into a soliloquy only marginally related to the topic. Some board members would shrink back in their seats, embarrassed by the content of the material Hanson insisted on sharing, but wondering if perhaps he had forgotten to take a particularly required dose of medication that day.

"Okay, let's return to our next item on the agenda, the spaghetti dinner fundraiser," Harold Mathers said, reclaiming control of the meeting. "We need to decide whether we want to partner with a company that will put our silent auction online...."

"I want to bring up the issue of whether board members can participate on the Center bowling team," Hanson interrupted. "Every time I bring this up, you keep putting it off, and I think I have the right to be heard on this...."

Mathers, board chair of the Iraq-Afghanistan Veterans Center of Harristown, a.k.a. Vet Center, was becoming less tolerant of humoring Hanson—even though everyone around the table knew that not alienating this boorish, crude man was necessary to maintain the good will of the Hanson Family Foundation.

The organization had begun with a Hanson Foundation startup grant. Now in its eighth year, the Vet Center had created a relatively stable diversification of its income stream, with the Foundation providing only about 10% of its annual revenue. The remainder came from state grants, fee for service payments from veterans who could afford to pay all or part of the costs, contributions from individuals, an annual spaghetti dinner fundraiser and silent auction, a $25,000 earmark provided courtesy of the state's senior U.S. senator out of the Veterans Administration budget, and a smattering of grants from other foundations. Still, 10% was 10%. In the Vet Center's budget, this amounted to $40,000, chump change for the Foundation, which had assets of more than $50 million.

The Vet Center conducted community outreach to offer counseling on employment, family issues, and education to returning combat veterans and family members. It also provided bereavement counseling for families of service members killed on active duty and counseling for veterans who were sexually harassed. Most of the Vet Center's services were offered on a sliding scale fee basis, although many programs were offered free of charge.

The center was staffed by small, mostly volunteer teams of counselors, outreach workers, and other specialists, including drug abuse counselors, advocates, and social workers trained in helping veterans access the full range of government-sponsored programs. A dedicated core staff of six full-time and four part-time professionals and support staff held everything together. Combat veterans in the area knew they could drop in to the Center, no questions asked, and play a round of pool in the recreation area and socialize. If

they decided to receive any vocational or mental health services, they could register, but there was no pressure to participate in the formal intake process if they simply wanted a
place to hang out.

Following years of military stalemate and only minimal
political progress, it appeared that there was no credible exit
strategy in America's overseas armed conflicts. It appeared
more and more likely that even with the election of a new
President who had pledged to bring them home as quickly as
possible, the number of veterans returning from overseas combat in that region had increased each year. The capacity of
the Vet Center to serve this demand was diminishing, even
with a healthy roster of volunteer caseworkers. As was the
case in many cash-strapped nonprofit organizations in the
area, the staff continually had been asked to do much more
with less. The current headquarters was straining beyond its
capacity, with some staff forced to have their desks in the
hallways with minimal space for the quiet and privacy necessary for the group and individual counseling staff members of
the Center provided.

Mathers and other members of the executive committee
had been making overtures to the Hanson Family Foundation
to provide a one-time grant of $500,000 so the organization
could purchase an office building in downtown Harristown
near the bus terminal and within a stone's throw of one of the
largest Army bases in the country. This would have been a
vast improvement over the current situation of renting space
that was expensive, inefficient, and had limited parking for
staff and clients.

Although Hanson had been an ally for this proposal, albeit with constant prodding from the committee, the family
members with control over funding had so far resisted increasing their investment in the organization. Yet, Mathers
thought progress had been made toward realizing the dream
whereby the Center could relocate to a modern facility that
could meet the needs for expansion for several decades into
the future. Even with all combat troops exiting from Iraq, the
war in Afghanistan was likely to expand, with no likelihood of
any negotiated political settlement nor possibility of a military solution, either. Even if the Vet Center board decided
against expanding its mission to provide services to those
veterans who were not returning combat veterans—as was

considered on occasion—it was almost a certainty that the organization would have a steady flow of new clients for many years to come.

For more than a year now, Mathers had debated with other board members on how to deal with this particular board member's deteriorating behavior. It was clear for a long time that Hanson attended every board meeting, but offered nothing constructive with his participation other than being the conduit for his relatives' philanthropy. The board previously had voted two other board members off simply for non-attendance, consistent with a provision in the organization's by-laws. At the last meeting, the board had surprised the current vice president of the board and charter board member with a plaque for recognizing his perfect attendance at each of the 50 board meetings in its history, the only board member with that distinction. Ironically, most board members would have voted in favor of some award for Hanson if he agreed simply *not* to attend any board meetings.

If the predicament had been limited to only Hanson's propensity for telling off-color jokes, the organization might have been able to weather the consequences. Anyone who spent any time around the Center would have been exposed to language that the nuns in the convent across the street would have blushed at.

But his vulgar behavior extended to verbal abuse, as well. Only an hour before, as lunch orders were being distributed, Hanson had bawled out a staff member for the insult of adding a sprinkling of onions on his hoagie sandwich when, Hanson had insisted, he had explicitly asked for no onions. In a gruff, hostile manner that was as much dog bark as human, Hanson had verbally pummeled the offender in front of the board and her executive director. The staff member, a young social work student doing her MSW program field placement who had volunteered to help out at the board meeting on what would otherwise have been a Saturday off, had been in tears. Two board members had tried to intercede, one of them protectively getting between Hanson and the student in case Hanson had any thoughts of physically attacking her. Although it never came to that, Mathers wondered whether the distinct, quick change from abusing the staff member to playfully telling a dirty joke might indicate some form of bipolar disorder.

And his appalling behavior extended beyond the six board meetings he attended each year.

Perhaps twice each month, Hanson would visit the Center and act as if he owned the place. He would order both staff and clients around as if they were his domestic help, and insist that as a board member, he had the right to examine the personal files of clients. When the executive director had calmly informed him that he could not have access to these files, Hanson had threatened to have the executive director fired at the next board meeting. Literally within the next five minutes, he had scolded one of the staff with a healthy dose of expletives mixed in to his ranting for refusing to agree to pick up his dry cleaning. As gently as they could, several staff members suggested he register for services himself so that he could participate in programs designed to help those like himself who were in need of a trained therapist to help him sort through his problems. Of course, he refused, railing against those who might suggest that he needed any kind of professional help.

At times, he seemed like a motor that wouldn't turn off, sharing comments during discussion that only marginally contributed to the board reaching a conclusion, if at all. During the few times that he was knowledgeable enough about an issue being discussed, he acted as if anyone who had a different opinion was either ignorant or plain stupid, and badgered those who refused to endorse his views until they were forced to show the white flag. It was clear to many on the board that his participation was not designed to serve the Vet Center but rather his own need for attention and power and to assuage whatever demons were inside his head.

Mathers might have forgiven the inappropriate outbursts to some reasonable extent. He, himself, had seen his share of bad things in Iraq, having led a platoon of infantrymen as a young second Lieutenant in Falusha, initially being a true believer hoping to rid the world of the evil dictator, Saddam Hussein. That idealism had inexorably melted away, replaced by a desire to do whatever he could to live another day and escape that hell-hole, the IEDs, and the constant sleep deprivation. Awarded the Bronze Star in 2004 for a Second Gulf War operation that he had difficulty discussing with others, he had returned and reentered civilian life a changed person.

Initially, he had experienced some adjustment problems, but he overcame them, unlike many of his buddies who still had neurons in their brains misfiring whenever they heard the mention of names like Nasiriyah, Debecka Pass, and Umm Qasr. Six years after being back in the States, he still flinched whenever he heard a car backfire. He had found and gotten involved with the Vet Center, and eventually was recruited to serve on the Center's board. Within a year, his quiet leadership merited a nomination as the board's fourth chair.

Hanson, also a veteran of the Persian Gulf War, the First Gulf War of 1990-1991, had seen combat more than a decade prior to Mathers. He had been awarded a Purple Heart and was in many ways emblematic of those individuals the Center sought to serve. Like many veterans, Hanson had seen and heard things during his service that he would have liked to forget. No one really knew whether he had received treatment for mental illness, but it was perceived that he had bouts of depression, alcoholism, and drug abuse following his return from overseas. Like thousands of his colleagues, he had experienced a puzzling array of symptoms, including headaches, joint pain, hair loss, memory loss, rashes, and unusual fatigue. The military had dismissed his symptoms as psychosomatic. It was only years later, as those with the symptoms had traded notes about their frustrations in receiving official Pentagon acknowledgement that they had real maladies, that Gulf War Syndrome was named. No cause was ever identified, and treatment remained elusive.

If Hanson was a sufferer of this syndrome, his outward symptoms were relatively mild compared to some of those who were served at the Vet Center. Yet, it was becoming increasingly clear that the board of the Vet Center was dysfunctional as long as Hanson continued to disrupt the board with his ill-timed outbursts, intimidation of other board members, and abuse of staff.

Had he simply been a filthy-mouthed fool, it might not have taken as much courage for Mathers or his predecessors to find a way to rotate him off the board gracefully without putting the Hanson Foundation funds going to the Vet Center at risk. But it wasn't that simple; there was some sympathy and compassion for Hanson's outrageous behavior that some within the organization thought may have been attributable to factors out of his own control, such as a physical chemical imbalance or a brain disturbance, or emotional problems emanating from his wartime experience.

Mathers had always treated Hanson with respect as a fellow combat veteran, and they were on good terms. It was assumed by the other board members that Mathers, both as someone with a good relationship with Hanson, and in his capacity of serving as chair, had the responsibility to deal with him.

Mathers had dealt successfully with disruptive board members before as chair of another organization. In one such case, he had scheduled a lunch meeting to discuss this, bringing along another member of the board for support.

He had begun by shaking hands warmly, making good eye contact, and calmly informing that board member that he and other members of the board had noticed behavior that might indicate that he was having problems outside of his board service, and that members were concerned about him. In any case, he had told the board member that there were times when he was interrupting too often and not focusing on the agenda. When he did so, the other board members were distressed, and the board was unable to do its job. Was there anything bothering him about the board that elicited the behavior that was of concern to the other members? It was important that every member have a chance to participate, and not feel uneasy about sharing their views. It was important for this board member to tone down the volume and try to listen more to what others had to say.

The board member, in this case, not only didn't become defensive, but apologized, and agreed to end his rudeness at board meetings. The rest of the meeting consisted of Mathers giving the board member some easily accomplishable assignments to keep him busy and reassuring him that he would continue to serve as a valued member of the board.

Instinctively, Mathers assessed that the outcome would be quite different if he employed the same strategy with Hanson, who would likely become defensive and create a scene, no matter how delicately Mathers handled the situation.

Perhaps they should meet in the park for lunch, with Mathers offering to bring some sandwiches and cold beer. He made a mental note that if he did so, he would be sure to not include onions in Hanson's sandwich.

Discussion Questions:

1. Who has the responsibility for dealing with disruptive board members?

2. How useful would it be to have a written policy on the roles and responsibilities of board members?

3. How much power do individual board members have when they visit the organization?

4. What is the role of staff in dealing with abusive and demanding board members?

5. Should Hanson simply be thrown off the board? What would be the consequences of doing so?

6. How can a board chair deal with a disruptive board member at a meeting and after a meeting?

7. Discuss the dilemma of dealing with maintaining the fiscal health of the center by protecting the funds it receives from the foundation while maintaining the functionality of the center and its board.

Case 11

Public Relations Dilemma at the Harristown Hospital and Health System

"This is Roemer," answered Steve Roemer, the Vice President for Public Affairs for the Harristown Hospital and Health System (HHHS), in response to his ringing Blackberry. He didn't recognize the number that flashed on his small screen. However, the area code of 404 indicated the call was from the Atlanta area.

It was 8:30 on a Monday evening, and he was in the middle of watching an episode of *House, MD.* The mythical Princeton Plainsboro Teaching Hospital didn't have much in common with HHHS, and he was aware that most medical staff at HHHS found the show ridiculous, particularly the main character's ethics, or lack thereof. Dr. House would have lasted no longer than a day on the staff of any real hospital, they asserted, regardless of whether he could save lives no one else could, all within a 43-minute timeframe plus commercials.

Reflexively, Roemer hit the pause button on the remote and took the call. Probably nothing that was needed of him that would be on the eleven o'clock news, he judged. Most of those calls involving a request for him to do a taped interview occurred during the early afternoon, for transmission back to the studio for editing in time for the six o'clock broadcast.

Roemer was proud of the fact that he made himself available 24/7 and was accessible to reporters working on deadline. While his smartphone might ring occasionally during the middle of the night, those times were rare. A former beat reporter for a South Carolina daily, he enjoyed the excitement of working with the media, particularly when he was sought out by television stations to appear live to comment on a breaking story. Health care was a broad, high-profile topic that would find itself often as a lead story in some context in the *Harristown Morning News,* and the television news, as well.

During the five years Roemer had served as the chief public relations professional of HHHS, he had developed substantial expertise on topics ranging from medical conditions and their treatment to the complexities of hospital finance and accounting. He had visions of returning to reporting, but he was also getting spoiled by the high salary and substantial fringe benefits and privileges of working in a corporate environment with staff and other resources to help him do his job. Whoever said working in the nonprofit sector guaranteed a low salary didn't know what they were talking about.

Occasionally, at the urging of his wife, he would turn off his Blackberry during "family time" and return any calls he received later. The advanced technology of the smartphone kept him connected, but he recognized that there was also a cost to being available day or night to not only reporters, but to his small staff and his superiors at HHHS. Unlike many other nonprofit organizations, this organization did not go to "sleep" after traditional business hours, although the pace may have appreciably diminished. There was a baseline of 8 a.m. to 4:30 p.m. office hours in the administrative floor of HHHS, with meetings, press conferences, production of the weekly newsletters, and preparing flashy briefing books for upcoming board meetings, filled with eye-catching graphics. But after business hours, the hospital remained a beehive of activity, with newsworthy developments periodically occurring in the evening, throughout the night, and on weekends, as well.

Other than perhaps the CEO, Roemer was the public face of the Health System, and that telegenic face had to remain clean-shaven because of the possibility that it would be on the other side of a camera with minimal notice.

It was Roemer's responsibility to keep the public educated and happy, and to have a positive association with the name of HHHS. Although generally no news was good news, Roemer proactively engaged the local media in covering aspects of hospital activities that would put it in a positive light. HHHS was an important pillar in the community—a respected player in the city's economic and social future, and second only to the state university as the largest employer in the city. It had a brand name to protect, and Roemer was its key frontline defender.

Despite its first-rate reputation, HHHS was in a constant competition for patients, who had a choice when deciding which among the three major acute care facilities in Harristown to patronize. (There had once been six hospitals in the community, but a series of mergers had resulted in HHHS absorbing three others in the 1990s.) Increasing market share was a key component of HHHS's strategic plan, and additional funds had been allocated to Roemer's department based on the premise that good public relations could improve that statistic, as well as improve its overall net revenue.

Despite its nonprofit status, improving net revenue was the principal focus of every management decision. The hospital typically charged its patients exorbitant fees for every procedure, as did the other two hospitals in the community. However, few patients paid the regular fee schedule; most charges were reimbursed by negotiated payments from private and government insurance. Even these rates were substantially higher than costs, so that treatment of nonpaying patients could be cross-subsidized. By state law, nonprofit hospitals were permitted to make a profit, but any net revenue over expenses was required to be funneled back for the hospital's charitable purposes. Those charitable purposes, of course, included investing in the most advanced technology, increasing staff salaries, and providing substantial perquisites to those who worked there, including the use of a Skybox at the NFL Stadium at the Sportsplex across town.

Roemer had attended several games seated in this box, enjoying a lavishly catered lunch and actively participating in the advocacy and fundraising carried on there directed at invited guests, such as the State's congressional delegation and potential donors. As a reporter, he had been able to purchase tickets to only a single Atlanta Falcons pre-season game during his five years at the paper, and he had paid for those seats himself.

In addition to his other responsibilities, Roemer was also part of the team of staff who decided which programs and activities would receive financial sponsorship of HHHS, with several million dollars available annually to support concerts, youth sports, museums, the Harristown Marathon, and other events that would help the community and provide more visibility and name recognition for HHHS. He really enjoyed this aspect of the job, using the Health System's money to benefit community groups.

Roemer's face had become familiar to TV viewers as a result of on-camera duties such as explaining the changing medical status of a celebrity admitted to the facility, updating the public about a train derailment that sent scores of injured to the hospital, or decrying a recent government report documenting an increase in the uninsured.

During one week two summers earlier, he had been a constant guest on all three local newscasts in the Harristown media market following a car accident involving the Mayor of Harristown. Mayor Hawkins had suffered a heart attack while at the wheel of his city-provided Honda Accord, careening into a telephone pole. Shortly after the accident, Roemer had appeared live from the scene of the accident, with five microphones thrust into his face, and reported that Mayor Hawkins was in stable condition, but that his Honda Accord was better described now as a Honda Accordion. People still stopped him to this day to express their appreciation for that quip.

In his position, there were a number of other opportunities he had to educate the public. It was not unusual for him to be stopped on the street and recognized as a celebrity himself. He was trusted by reporters, although he certainly provided a spin on his comments that was flattering to his employer. No one would have expected anything else.

Now that he had built up a good reputation as a straight shooter, reporters came to him for both on the record and off the record comments. He liked his job. He liked being a part of the decision-making as part of the management team that ran the hospital, even though that was not a formal part of his job description. Most of the Vice Presidents, along with the President and CEO, had been there only a few years, and he felt that they valued the institutional memory he brought along with his common sense about how the public and other stakeholders might respond to consequences of a decision.

More than a few times, his advice prevented the management team from taking action that might have been a disaster. Today, however, he had been frustrated that the CEO and Vice Presidents failed to recognize the seriousness of their decision with respect to one particular sensitive matter involving a young surgeon, who was fired for attempting to perform an operation while heavily intoxicated. In this case, the doctor had been partying late into the night, but had been on call. When he responded to a page to come in to perform an emergency appendectomy, operating room nurses had complained that he was not in any condition to operate. Fortunately, another surgeon was available to fill in, and the patient had a normal procedure, unaware of the situation that might have put her at serious risk.

This was the second time the doctor had had a problem with alcohol interfering with his duties. The Medical Director had no second thoughts about firing him, and did so. However, the doctor knew that being fired for alcohol abuse would make it virtually impossible for him to be hired at another hospital. So, this doctor threatened to go public with allegations of gross negligence on the part of hospital staff, resulting in the deaths of two patients the previous year, unless the HHHS complied with a series of demands.

Apparently, hospital staff had participated in a cover-up involving a medical error. In that case, two children had been provided with lethal doses of heparin, a commonly used blood thinner, by hospital personnel. A similar medical error had made the national news in 2007 when a child of actor Dennis Quaid had barely survived such an overdose. The error was compounded by a defect in the package labeling, which failed to distinguish adequately between the weak dose administered to children and the standard dose administered to adults, which was 1,000 times more potent. After considering whether or not to disclose the medical error to the children's parents, the hospital staff had decided to simply explain to the families of the victims that the two patients had died from causes unrelated to injecting these kids with a lethal overdose. And it had issued strict verbal instructions to all staff involved in the incident to keep their mouths shut about what happened.

What the surgeon now demanded was that the hospital would have to provide him with a letter of recommendation and agree not to disclose to anyone outside of the hospital management that he had been fired or the reasons why. Second, the hospital would have to provide him with a severance payment of $500,000, which would automatically become

$5,000,000, payable at the rate of $500,000 each year, if anyone in the hospital violated the first provision.

The management team had met that afternoon to decide whether or not to approve the agreement.

Roemer was hearing this story for the first time today, and he was uncomfortable. Had he been in charge, he would not have covered anything up. He would have explained the error and let the chips fall where they may. His experience was that many people understood that errors are made by professionals in all fields, although the consequences of errors in the medical field are certainly more serious than, let's say, allowing a ground ball to go through one's legs during a baseball game. But unlike a baseball game where the mistake is seen and understood by everyone in the stands, medical errors often occur without anyone knowing about them other than the staff. And the consequences can be fatal for the patient. There is a huge incentive for the staff to keep mistakes they make from the patients and their families, avoiding a lot of unpleasantness in addition to civil liability that can amount to millions of dollars in any single case.

At an afternoon meeting, where this situation was discussed among a small group of management with the chief counsel present, the team had decided to minimize the hospital's potential exposure and accept the surgeon's offer. Roemer had been the sole dissenter, arguing that the hospital should acknowledge its mistakes, suffer the consequences of being accountable for its mistakes, and not give in to what he perceived was blackmail. The chief counsel had been neutral on the decision, although she did point out that in the event this doctor was hired by another hospital and was involved in a similar incident, the fact that HHHS failed to take appropriate action rather than covering it up could make HHHS potentially liable.

Roemer was moving up the ladder in leadership of the Council of Hospital Public Relations Professionals, in line to become its next chair. The Council had an ethics code, which Roemer took seriously. Among the provisions of this code was an obligation to be accurate and truthful in representing the interests of one's employer to the public, as well as an obligation to serve the public interest. In Roemer's twelve years as information officer, he had never knowingly lied to the media or the public about a professional issue. He knew that this would be severely tested if anyone ever raised the issue of either the medical error cover-up or the agreement HHHS management had just agreed to make with the terminated surgeon.

Although the decision made at the meeting made Roemer uncomfortable, it certainly wasn't the first time that decisions made at the highest levels of HHHS were inconsistent with his personal and professional values. However, he recognized that he was not the boss, and that overall, HHHS, despite some flaws, was operated in a manner to serve the public. And he never lied about anything, although he occasionally would tell a reporter that he was not free to comment on a particular situation.

With the TV paused, Roemer listened to the voice at the other end of the line.

"Hi, this is Steve Barton. I'm with the Associated Press in Atlanta, and I am working on a story for AP about HHHS. I'm calling with a couple questions. We are working on a story involving problems with the blood thinner Heparin, which had some problems relating to contamination, as well as overdosing. One of our sources referred us to your hospital, which apparently ran into a problem with heparin overdoses last year. While researching this, we came across a story of a surgeon from HHHS who was terminated today for attempting to operate on a patient while impaired with alcohol, and found out that there was some relationship between these two incidents, which we are not clear about. Can you clarify some of this for me? I understand that you were at the meeting today at HHHS where this was discussed...."

Discussion Questions:

1. How should a public relations professional deal with any conflict between the principles of one's professional ethics code and the exigencies required to represent the interests of one's organization?

2. Is Roemer obligated to talk to the reporter about the meeting? How should he respond?

3. What boundaries should individuals have between their personal lives and professional lives?

4. Is there anything unethical or otherwise inappropriate about HHHS having a Skybox for entertaining VIPs?

5. Was the decision to agree to the terms of the surgeon appropriate? What other options did the management of HHHS have?

6. If a staff member of a nonprofit is fired for misconduct, is it ethical not to take steps to inform any potential future employer of that staff member that the person has engaged in misconduct?

7. Could the hospital management have had any other options other than firing the surgeon?

8. Compare and contrast two very different types of charities that may be headquartered in the same neighborhood, such as a hospital and a food bank.

Case 12

Approving a Partnership Agreement— Board Paralysis at the State Association

Steve Miller, Executive Director of the State Association of County and Municipal Officials (SACMO), was so frustrated by his board's inability to make a final decision, he would have pulled his hair out. Not that doing so would have been literally possible, as his head was as smooth and hairless as a baby's bottom. He was often called "Mr. Clean" around the office, and it wasn't because of his ethical perspective, which was otherwise exemplary, but rather because of his resemblance to the cartoon character that was used for decades to sell the famous household cleaning product.

Each time SACMO's full board met and considered the revised version of the partnering agreement with an online job board vendor, Miller had to re-explain, almost from the beginning, what the proposal involved, why it was taking so long, what the objections were to the previous version, what the response was from the vendor to the suggested changes to the contract, and what input SACMO's pro bono attorney provided on the issue. This then opened up the full range of issues in the agreement for debate one more time.

He knew that some of the concerns raised by his board were valid. But he also felt that many of these problems could be worked out easily on the fly outside of the contractual process. It would be impossible to anticipate every imaginable hypothetical situation that might actually come up once the job board became operational. Miller did not feel that his board appreciated the fact that there had to be at least some measure of trust between parties to a partnering agreement, or there would never be an end to the process of creating the language that would cover all conceivable contingencies.

The vendor, Harbaugh JobBoard Services, was established and reputable; there were almost 400 other state and national associations that were currently in a contractual partnership with Harbaugh. There was no evidence that Harbaugh had ever violated any of the existing partnering agreements, and Miller had verified that there was general satisfaction with the services the firm provided.

Miller had already been informed by Jeff White, Harbaugh's marketing staff associate, that the company's patience had a limit, and that perhaps another association with related interests, such as the League of State Municipal Workers, would be more responsive to Harbaugh's time constraints. Although the vendor understood the restrictions on what Miller could do unilaterally, there had to be some deadline placed on the process if SACMO was to continue to be a viable partner with them on the project, or they would be forced to withdraw. Each unnecessary cycle of board meeting, re-referral to a committee, and renegotiation with Harbaugh meant the loss of revenue that was expected from the new Web site. With the clock ticking, it also became more likely that competitive job board sites, spearheaded by Harbaugh's competitor, would capture whatever market SACMO would be seeking beyond that of its own membership. If that had been permitted to occur, both SACMO and Harbaugh would suffer the consequences.

Miller had been quite excited when he had received an unsolicited e-mail more than two years earlier from Harley Harbaugh, founder and president of Harbaugh JobBoard Services, proposing a potential partnership. Harbaugh was the second largest vendor of online job boards in the country and was in a struggle with one other for-profit company for expanding its reach in niché markets. Harbaugh and its fierce rival were engaging in cut-throat competition, with both companies aggressively seeking to partner with large state associations in all 50 states, seeking to maximize market share.

At the moment, each vendor sought to recruit as many associations as possible to its client list, offering very favorable terms to them, even if there might be a short-term net loss of revenue to the vendors by doing so. Both firms recognized a benefit in signing up as many associations as they could, if only to keep them out of the clutches of their rival.

In the long run, each expected that only one would survive. Both vendors assumed they had to take reckless chances, knowing that failure would result in the demise of one or the other company and losses for the banks and venture capitalists that had taken a chance on their competing business models.

The associations that they were enticing to be their customers, in contrast, operated in a completely different environment. Few had any fear that a rival would spring up out of nowhere and take away their members. Most had existed for decades and operated with a mix of income from membership dues; fees for services; the sale of publications, Web site advertising, and mailing lists; partnerships with vendors who sold discounted insurance, affinity credit cards, and publications; and grants. Major decisions involving commercial partnerships were made by the full board at quarterly board meetings. These might occur as long as four months apart, depending on the season of the year.

For some vendors, three months to make a decision was incomprehensible, and some explicitly avoided partnering agreements with the nonprofit sector because of this difference in culture. Others found these association-based markets to be so lucrative that they suffered through the inevitable delays and the potential for stillborn agreements after hundreds of hours of fruitless wooing of potential partners and negotiating contracts that were never signed.

Miller had spent considerable time researching Harbaugh and its major competition, consulting his colleagues who were executive directors at other state associations that had job boards. He found that what Harbaugh was proposing made perfect sense, and that the initial terms of the offer were much better than what Harbaugh's competition was currently offering. After his initial positive response to Harbaugh's e-mail invitation, Miller had been assigned to work with Jeff White, a Harbaugh marketing associate, for further details.

Within a few weeks, he got back to White and let him know that SACMO was interested, and that they should meet. White proposed meeting the next day, but Miller was quite busy dealing with an upcoming board meeting and a statewide conference. So, they had scheduled a lunch meeting for three weeks later to discuss how the proposal would work.

Miller was excited about the proposal, as setting up a job board on the SACMO Web site was one of the tasks that was on his list of things to do when operations got a bit less hectic. But knowing that there was limited time to pursue every good idea, Miller had put this on the back burner so as to carve out more time to resolve other, more pressing, problems that were required to be addressed.

To have a reputable company with a stellar track record approach him and have the capacity and expertise to remove all of the barriers was a major coup for his association. And one of the most attractive features of the offer was that Harbaugh had a template that would work quite well with the Web design SACMO already had in place.

White estimated that his technical staff could begin work right away once the contract was signed, and it might only take 15-30 days before the job board would be up and running, customized to look exactly like other Web pages on the SACMO site and with all of the features customized in accordance with their agreement.

Harbaugh was making an offer to Miller for a collaboration that would be on terms that would be quite beneficial to SACMO, provide it with guaranteed revenue, and provide a new, attractive member benefit. Harbaugh proposed to integrate a state-of-the-art job board within SACMO's Web site, handle all back-office operations such as technical support (using an 800 number), billing, collections (always a difficult aspect of any entrepreneurial endeavor), and Web design, and provide a substantial percentage of the revenue the job board generated to SACMO.

Adding a state-of-the-art job board, such as the platform designed by Harbaugh, had been a goal of Miller for several years. As envisioned by Miller, there would be a Web page on the SACMO site for members to post job opportunities. He had considered the costs to the organization of managing the software; posting the jobs; and handling the billing, customer service, technical service, and collections. It seemed overwhelming to do all of this in-house. He had given little thought to the possibility that such a site might have the potential to generate net revenue, considering the staff time that would be needed to provide for its care and feeding.

But even he had to admit that the comprehensive job board and career services offered by Harbaugh came with nifty standard bells and whistles that were well beyond his imagination. Of course, there would be job postings, easily posted by organizations seeking job candidates without the need for anyone from SACMO to be involved, with payments made by credit card or PayPal processed online. SACMO, if it so desired, could delete any postings that it deemed were inappropriate, or that were not for jobs with local governments in the state. The entire process, from posting to billing, would be completely automated.

In addition, the site would have links to hundreds of articles, in a searchable format, providing career advice, résumé preparation services commissionable to SACMO, courses that would be certified for continuing education and commissionable to SACMO if the purchase was generated by clicks on SACMO's job board pages, and career-related blogs moderated by experts. Job seekers could sign up for e-mail job alerts, letting them know when a new job was posted that fit their profile.

Job seekers could post their résumés with privacy, and prospective employers would be able to view these résumés without contact information, requiring the permission of the job seeker to view the contact details. And when the employer received that permission and paid a reasonable fee, a modest payment would be deposited directly into SACMO's account.

All services would be free to job seekers, and job posters would pay a posting charge with more than half the revenue going to SACMO for jobs posted by SACMO members. The site would also include jobs posted by non-members who paid to have their job listings posted on the SACMO site, commissionable to SACMO.

A marketing and sales team at Harbaugh was working full-time to convince job posters from all over the country to post on the network. When job posters chose to include their job postings on the SACMO job board, which they could do by a simple check box from a list of job boards on the Harbaugh network, a portion of their fees would be provided to SACMO. And when a SACMO member organization included its posting on boards on that network other than the SACMO job board site, SACMO would receive a share of the fee above what the organization would receive if the job had appeared only on the SACMO online job board.

Harbaugh proposed to customize the job board Web pages to look exactly like other pages of the SACMO site, at no cost. Most importantly, Harbaugh would handle all of the work involved, including customer service, billing, collections, and technical assistance. SACMO would maintain complete control over many of the site's features, such as the ability to set prices and provide discounts to members.

The attractive content included on the career site pages would generate traffic from a wide range of individuals. Site visitors would be able to view banner and button ads at the option of the association. If it chose that option, the revenue from these ads would be shared, based on which party generated the ad sale. A year earlier, SACMO had insisted that it be able to screen ads for appropriateness, and within two hours of being informed about that request, White had e-mailed back a modification of the agreement language to permit that right.

Although Harbaugh had initially asked for a five-year contract, the firm had agreed to a two-year deal at the insistence of the SACMO board.

The only fly in the ointment was the inability of Miller to shepherd the final approval through his board process. It was not for lack of motivation; Miller felt completely hamstrung by all of the hoops that had to be navigated. As soon as he thought he had finally brought the process to a conclusion, another objection was raised by one board member or another that stymied his effort to get the authorization he needed to get the contract signed and the partnership finally operational.

Unfortunately, neither Miller nor White and his organization could have anticipated the problems of getting the contract formally approved by the association. It was a nightmare. Had the decision-making rested entirely with the executive director, the entire process might have taken only a few months.

Even this amount of time was far longer than what one would expect had the organization been a for-profit, with executive decision-making centralized entirely in the hands of the CEO. But as an executive director of a federally tax-exempt 501(c)(6) nonprofit association, and a board of directors whose members were not always on the same page with respect to primary mission and goals, it was not unusual for decisions to take much longer than their for-profit counter-parts. In this case, with a board of directors consisting pri-marily of elected officials who reveled in exercising their power to micro-managing many aspects of the organization, Miller was unable to consummate the deal internally, despite the enthusiasm within his organization for doing so quickly with the vendor.

At each meeting, the Harbaugh collaboration would be first on the agenda under "Old Business." And at each meet-ing, there was some small detail about the partnering agree-ment that sabotaged final ratification of the agreement, re-quiring Miller to go back to Harbaugh to seek one minor change or another, and then report back at the next quarterly board meeting. Or, at times, the board deputized its Planning Com-mittee to agree that whatever concern raised at the board meeting, legitimate or otherwise, was sufficiently addressed to recommend signing the agreement.

Complicating the approval was the fact that the Plan-ning Committee had serious problems of its own. Two staff members, each with responsibilities for staffing the commit-tee, had resigned successively within six months of joining the staff, taking with them much of the institutional memory for this particular partnership. Miller had been forced to take over the Harbaugh contract negotiations while he was en-gaged in finding replacements for those staff members, and this further delayed consideration by the Planning Commit-tee of the changes the board had asked to be made to the agreement. During the time period when there had been no Planning Committee staff member, no staff from SACMO was communicating with Harbaugh, and the Planning Committee had decided not to meet, further delaying the process.

After two years of this on again, off again process, Harbaugh was quite resigned to recognizing that SACMO was unwilling or unable to reach an agreement. White was quite patient, but two years of accommodating SACMO's needs about agreement provisions that were quite unlikely to ever need to be enforced was wearing him down. Other associations he had worked with during the past five years had also had this irritating aspect of their governance, but only SACMO's lack of ability to "get to yes" appeared to him to be pathological and needing the equivalent of organization therapy.

For his part, Miller could only apologize profusely for each delay and explain that his board consisted of individual personalities who were oblivious to the irrational requirements they placed on partnering agreements with third parties. He continually explained that his board's disability was not directed against Harbaugh itself, but rather was symptomatic of its dysfunctional approach to decision-making. He considered guaranteeing that the board would complete action on the contract at the next meeting, but he knew in his heart that doing so would be making a promise he likely would be unable to honor.

At one point in this process, Miller had joked with his wife that he was hopeful that the job board would become available soon with or without the participation of SACMO, as he would be one of the first to utilize its services to find a new professional opportunity in his field. As he sat in his board meeting today, enduring yet another likely postponement of the decision, that flight of whimsy almost a year earlier seemed less capricious and more like a plan.

At this moment, as Miller was reflecting on the storied history of this agreement, the board was ponderously moving closer to delaying approval once again. The motion on the floor was to refer the contract back to the Planning Committee to come up with revisions to the contract on a provision that had twice before been revised by that committee, and had already been approved by the board almost four board meetings ago—before a nascent issue had derailed the process. At the request of a single board member who had been newly elected to the board in the interim, the full board had agreed that there might be some situation, however remote, in which Harbaugh JobBoard might gain a small windfall if a peculiar set of circumstances occurred. In any case, the board member had insisted that the provision be clarified and the board was poised to give its assent to that demand, referring the contract back to the Planning Committee.

The chair of the board, a small-town mayor from the rural, western part of the state, was not particularly interested in having an association online job board. He recruited his small staff from his large campaign contributors and their relatives, his own relatives, and his personal friends. However, he recognized that there was some enthusiasm from the association's staff and from other members of the board to pursue this opportunity. But as for devoting any political capital in moving the process to a conclusion, he didn't feel that this was particularly a good investment. The chair also was an opponent of an effort by the board to hire an attorney on staff to deal with the myriad legal problems that came before the association, including partnering agreements, contracts, leases, and liability issues. Instead, he had offered the services of an attorney who was one of his campaign contributors who, for a reduced fee, would review these matters.

This saved the association legal expenses. But it also delayed most legal matters involving the association, because this particular attorney did not make the association business a priority as she would have done had the association been a full-paying client.

This was not the first time that the board had thrown a monkey-wrench into Miller's plans to partner with an online vendor. Several years earlier, he had been approached by a firm that designed online shopping malls. The partnership had never been approved by the board. By the time the Planning Committee and the board had felt satisfied that there was an air-tight agreement between the two parties, the vendor had gone belly-up. In retrospect, the fact that this deal never was executed was unimportant, but Miller began to understand why those in the for-profit sector often demur when trying to work with their counterparts in the nonprofit sector. He came to realize that one of the great advantages of being an entrepreneur was the ability to make decisions quickly without much second-guessing. Power within a nonprofit organization, by comparison, was much more diffuse.

Meanwhile, Miller sat at the board meeting silently. He debated whether to explain to the board that he needed to find some way to maintain Harbaugh's interest in working with SACMO. Otherwise, Harbaugh would likely pull out.

Miller recognized that his evaluation and annual contract was on the board agenda for the following meeting, and he hesitated to vocalize another protest of what he judged to be another unnecessary delay in approving the Harbaugh partnering agreement. Once his new contract was signed, he perhaps could be a bit more aggressive in serving as an advocate for approval of the final version, he rationalized—that is, if Harbaugh was willing to accept yet another delay.

Discussion Questions:

1. How much power should nonprofit organization executive directors have to commit their organizations to partnership agreements without involvement of their boards of directors?

2. What changes might SACMO make in its governance structure to avoid situations that would make it hamstrung to enter into partnerships and collaborations in the future?

3. What are some of the reasons why it may be appropriate for a nonprofit corporation and a for-profit corporation to have a different standard entering into a partnership agreement with respect to timelines and the extent to which decision-making is decentralized among various stakeholders within the organization?

4. What are some of the procedures and policies a nonprofit organization might follow if approached by a for-profit company with a proposal to enter into a partnership with respect to determining whether the for-profit is legitimate, stable, and able to deliver on its promises?

5. Is there anything inappropriate about the association retaining the services of an attorney who has a less than arms-length relationship with the chair of the board of directors?

Case 13

The State Volunteer Firefighters Association's Dilemma

"Okay, I think everyone is on the call," intoned Chief Jake Weber, the crusty board chair of the State Volunteer Firefighters Association, who had served as the chair for almost 30 years. Weber had called the emergency meeting of the Association's executive board to discuss how to respond to ethics charges made against the association's executive director, Abraham Firth, by the board's current Vice President, Harold Sanders. Weber had scheduled the call with reluctance, concerned about the allegations made against the executive director, but willing to give him the benefit of the doubt. After all, for the past 20 years, Firth had been the face of volunteer firefighting in the state, and his service to the association had been exemplary.

In two decades, Firth had transformed the association from a near-bankrupt, moribund and disorganized collective into a powerful force within the first responder community in the state. He was a visible presence not only statewide, but on the national scene, as well. Whenever there was a national issue of prominence that might benefit from the expertise of someone in the volunteer firefighting community, Firth was the "go to" guy. He had made several appearances on CNN, made a short appearance in one *60 Minutes* segment, and could be counted on to deliver the association's message with the most appropriate and credible spin to state and Congressional lawmakers. Perhaps a dozen times each year, he would walk up the steps of the State Capitol and deliver testimony to various House and Senate committees, embedded with a catchy sound bite that never failed to capture the media's attention and make the evening newscasts.

Unlike many executive directors who turned over day-to-day operations to their staff, Firth was a hands-on executive director who sweated all of the details. He was worshiped by his staff, and he treated them with respect from the CFO to the receptionist. When they grew professionally, he encouraged them to find more challenging employment and continued to mentor them. More than a handful of volunteer fire companies in the state were administered by those who had first learned the business at Firth's knee.

Firth gave no indication that he was unhappy with his job or the firefighting profession in general. He was usually the first person in the office and the last to leave, and he never complained about being on call 24/7 to respond to organizational exigencies. And as a volunteer firefighter himself for more than 30 years, he knew all of the issues affecting his constituency from firsthand experience. He and Chief Weber had served as a team for two decades. Weber was the chief of a VFC in a rural area upstate and had his hands full. He knew the association's management was in capable hands, and he let Firth run the association without any micromanaging from him. Although they occasionally disagreed on policy, they worked things out quickly without any rancor. They considered each other friends.

So it was with extreme consternation and surprise when the word filtered throughout the volunteer firefighting community that someone had written a "tell all" book about his experiences within the volunteer firefighting community. The author was someone named "David Getty," and it was determined that no one by that name was known to anyone and it was likely to be a pseudonym. To old timers in the state, some of the stories sounded familiar. Only a few people in the entire country would have known about them. Extrapolating, it became clear to those who read the pirated galley of the soon-to-be-published book that had appeared mysteriously on an obscure Web site that only Firth could have written it. It had appeared on the site frequented by firefighters for only a day, in PDF format, and had disappeared just as mysteriously as it had appeared. But by then, it had been downloaded by several site visitors and was virally being circulated by the hundreds among the community of first responders.

When confronted, Firth refused to either confirm or deny the allegation, saying that it was not anyone's business.

Several board members were livid when they heard this, and Chief Weber had been deluged with calls and e-mails from not only irate members of his board but from staff of the volunteer fire companies that were members of the association. Weber was convinced himself that Firth was the author. And he was equally convinced that although the book would do damage to the profession if and when it was published and made available to the public, it also cast a positive light on the importance of volunteer fire companies in society, the bravery of individuals serving their communities, and the intensity of the training most members of VFCs receive. He was disappointed in several rants that appeared in the book about petty politics. And there was certainly nothing positive about the many cases described in detail in the manuscript of scandalous, and at times illegal, behavior that had been covered up.

But it was a damn good read! At times, Weber felt, he could almost smell the black, acrid smoke, and experience the adrenalin rush of racing off to a call, not knowing if it was a false alarm—as many calls were—or a serious emergency that conjured up the images of that 1991 movie *Backdraft,* which gave the public a glimpse of the heart-pounding tension involved in operations of the Chicago FD.

The outrage of those who communicated to Weber was accompanied by suggestions on how to discipline Mr. Firth for the breach of confidentiality and protocol. Other than simple outright calls for his immediate firing unless he agreed to take whatever steps deemed necessary to stop publication of the book, the board chair was called upon to require that Firth's advance and royalties related to the book become the property of the association. The justification was that all of the stories and information shared by Mr. Firth came from sources that were related to his highly paid, professional position at the association or his previous position as the administrator of a VFC.

Another board member suggested that these were ill-gotten gains, and that Firth had a conflict of interest. Knowing that he was planning to write a book, his interest in serving the association's membership was in conflict with his interest in generating titillating material that he could exploit to spike book sales, which may have colored his judgments about decision-making.

Another board member suggested that even if the book had been complimentary to the association and the profession, Firth had no right to take advantage of his position to generate his own personal wealth while he was employed professionally by the association. At a minimum, in order to access confidential records and sensitive matters, he was ethically required to obtain permission from the board, as those who shared information with him were doing so with the expectation that his access to information was predicated on the assumption that he was serving the interests of the association and its members rather than himself. In addition, the property of the association was not intended to be exploited for the personal gain of anyone, but rather intended for the exclusive use of serving the interests of the association.

Of particular concern to several board members was the fact that their executive director had publicly shared stories that embarrassed the association and the volunteer firefighting profession as a whole.

The downloaded galley Weber had reviewed revealed bombshells dropping with each page turn. There were stories of hazing of new members. There were accounts of VFCs discovering that some within their ranks had purposely set fires, and that they had participated in cover-ups of these crimes. There were stories of sexual harassment, and even sexual assault, of female volunteers. Volunteers were recruited who were under the state-mandated legal minimum age of 18. Prostitutes were hired to attend a members-only beer bash sponsored by one local VFC.

Also documented were tales of financial mismanagement and outright fraud, theft, and embezzlement. Racism, sexism, and anti-Semitism were highlighted, certainly scourges perhaps disproportionately affecting those who lived in many small towns that relied on the services of volunteer firefighters. These discrimination incidents were often magnified in rural areas that did not have the opportunity for diversity training, which might have been available in urban communities that might be more welcoming to those who were not of the "right" race or religion. Or, perhaps in just the past 20 years, the "right" gender. Women only recently had been forcibly integrated into the ranks of firefighting, and many firefighting organizations resisted this change in the culture that was forced upon them by federal laws. Women either gave up or suffered in silence. The book provided details of some of the most egregious cases of hazing of women volunteers.

But the most compelling and horrifying stories involving discrimination against volunteer firefighters revolved around what some firefighters did to those who they either knew or suspected were gay. One story centered upon one volunteer who had communicated no evidence relating to his sexual orientation, but who disliked football and liked Broadway show music, leading to stereotyped speculations about his sexuality. What his colleagues did to him to show their distaste would turn the movie about this book from a PG-13 to an R rating, if it ever did become a movie, which appeared to be a distinct possibility. The salaciousness of some of the stories made it quite possible that someone would find bidding on the book's movie rights to be attractive.

For his part, the author had made it clear that most volunteer firefighters were patriotic, hard-working, and put service to their communities paramount. There was nothing in the book that condoned the inappropriate behavior. There was little in the book that the board members who were either volunteer firefighters or who worked with them professionally found surprising, likely to have been embellished, or fabricated.

The fact that this book was likely to have been written by Firth gave credibility to stories they read that they were hearing for the first time. Yet there was something unsettling for those in the firefighting community to find out that it was one of their own who was responsible for what was likely to be a public relations nightmare. If published, the book would likely cast a cloud over the profession that would impugn the integrity of the majority for the actions of a small minority.

After Weber determined who was present, he launched a discussion of the matter at hand and what should be done.

"This is Felicia. I actually enjoyed reading the book. But I see two distinct issues that are problematic with this situation," commented Dr. Felicia Howser, an associate professor for the State University who was a specialist in nonprofit law and ethics and the only female on the board. "The first issue, which is of paramount concern, is the potential, if not actual, conflict of interest, involved in Abe being involved at all in writing this book.

"We are paying him to be a staff member, and we should expect that this creates a requirement of loyalty to the organization. He has an obligation to represent our interests publicly and be discreet with how he shares information that he receives in the course of his job that we have a right to expect should be kept confidential. When he writes this book, it creates a dual relationship on his part.

"He has to choose between whether to represent the interests of the publisher and make the book interesting enough to generate substantial sales, or whether he represents the interests of the organization that pays his salary. There may be a value to the readers to consider his thoughts on these issues that are internal to the Association. But it certainly doesn't have much value to us to have our dirty laundry aired in public.

"The second issue is, even if we were to require that we approve the book in advance, there is a question in my mind as to whether the income derived from this activity belongs to Abe."

"Hightower here. I think any money generated by this book belongs to the Association," chimed in Gregg Hightower, a VFC administrator from Oshman, on the east coast of the state. "If he made money playing in a rock band, the money would clearly be his. But in this case, he is taking obviously confidential and sensitive information that he would otherwise not have any access to and making money from telling the world about it. But even if he gives us the money, I think he should be fired regardless. He's made some of us look like immature fraternity boys, and it is not fair for us to be paying him a cent more. I want to be on record that if he isn't fired soon, Oshman VFC will put its Association dues payment in escrow until he is fired."

"This is Vinnie Altman from Troy VFC. Gregg has a good point, although I don't see what we would accomplish by firing Abe, who by consensus is a terrific executive director. I don't see the possibility of finding anyone better to replace him. But I do see the need to discipline him for the breach of confidentiality. I suggest we let him know that we think this book violated the confidentiality of our association, and that we move to suspend him for two weeks without pay."

"At this point, we don't know definitively that he wrote the book, although his fingerprints are certainly on the passages I read," interrupted Harry Sanger, in a booming bass voice that was so distinct and unusually loud that no one required him to first identify himself before his comment. "Jake is a good friend of his; maybe the two of them can sit down, have Jake explain why we are so pissed at this, and see if Abe himself is willing to admit that perhaps writing this book while still employed by us was not such a good idea. Maybe he is willing to voluntarily donate all or part of the proceeds to some charity as a sign of good faith, or better still, simply inform the publisher that he has had a change in heart and is withdrawing the book from consideration."

"This is Williams," intoned Tom Williams, a driver of a hook-and-ladder for Griffin VFC. "I think we should fire the S.O.B. He violated our trust. I don't know how I can have a private conversation with him in the future about a sensitive matter without thinking that he is taking notes and I'll read about it in his next book."

"I'll talk to Abe, as Harry suggested, but I think it is wishful thinking to expect that this book will never be published in substantially the form that we have seen. But maybe we can use our influence to have it toned down a bit. Anyway, I think we do not have any consensus within the executive committee," summarized Chief Weber. "So I will put this on the agenda at the next board meeting in two months. By then, maybe I'll have more information about what actually happened and some more options on what we can do about it. In the meantime, thank you all for participating, and I'll see you at the board meeting."

Everyone took this as the cue to hang up, other than Williams.

"Jake, you've got to deal with this; that's why we pay you the big bucks to be the chair. Make it right."

"I hear you, buddy. I'm not happy about this book, either, but as you can tell from this call, there is no clear consensus on what to do, and the options we have are limited. Even if we fire him, as you suggest, we could be hit with a lawsuit for wrongful discharge, and it could cost us plenty in legal fees even if we won. Let me talk with Abe, and see if I can resolve this to your satisfaction. Firing him doesn't help anyone, and I think the best interests of the association would suffer, although I see your point about needing to talk to Abe without the conversation appearing in print."

"Okay, Jake. Regards to Wilma."

"Regards to Althea, and let's get together after the board meeting and check out that new restaurant on Almand Street."

"Bye, my friend."

"Bye."

Discussion Questions

1. What constraints can/should a nonprofit organization put on the behavior of its executive director related to how that individual spends his or her free time?

2. Is there an implied requirement that a nonprofit employee act with loyalty to an organization that employs him/her?

3. Who has the authority to fire an executive director: the board, the executive committee, the board chair?

4. What could the board have done to avoid this situation?

5. Did the executive director in this case act unethically?

6. Does the organization have any claim to the money the executive director received for writing this book?

7. Is it a problem for any organization to have the same board chair for decades? What are the pros and cons of permitting this?

Case 14

The One (Wo)Man Band Running the Kenmore Midget Baseball League

Looking at a street light outside the second story window of the Clubhouse, Sarah determined that it was still snowing lightly. The Borough's maintenance crew had plowed out the parking lot in Kenmore Borough Park in response to her telephone request earlier that day, as she had expected. No one else would have thought to make that call, she mused, and there might have been no place for cars to park otherwise because of the foot of snow that had fallen earlier in the week. *Without me, this organization would be only a skeleton of what it is now,* she thought.

A couple of cars were still pulling into the parking lot of the Clubhouse, but Sarah prided herself on starting board meetings exactly on time.

With two minutes to go before the digital clock in the Clubhouse hit 7 p.m., Sarah imagined how the scene outside of this window would be different six months hence, the sun still relatively high in the sky and the temperature hovering in the low '90s, perhaps 70 degrees warmer than it was now. She could almost smell the pungent odor of the mustard that would be spread liberally atop the soft pretzels sold from the concession stand housed in the Clubhouse's first floor, the pretzels often stale, soggy, and delicious!

She delighted in the smell of the freshly mowed grass, the baseball diamond manicured with care by her two sons.

Among the sounds were a cacophony of dogs barking, babies crying in their mothers' arms, the chatter of players shouting encouragement to their teammates, and parents and coaches shouting out instructions. And, of course, the occasional "pong" of aluminum striking a ball. "Swing, batter!"

In the scene she conjured up, there were also younger siblings of the players ignoring the action on the field, instead playing tag with each other or catching lightning bugs and grasshoppers, the latter to use as bait to catch sunfish in Kenmore Creek. Midget League, for kids 10-12, was truly an intergenerational activity. Grandparents, and even great-grandparents, would attend games, some making the trip from the parking lot to the temporary stands using walkers.

Her reverie was interrupted by her Blackberry chiming the tune "Take Me Out to the Ball Game," indicating that it was 7 p.m. and time to start the meeting.

"The board meeting will come to order," announced Sarah Goodling, banging the ceremonial gavel that was presented to her at a board meeting of the Kenmore Midget Baseball League, Inc. two years ago. Two more parents entered the room as she spoke. They quietly took seats around the large folding table and reached in the center of the table for a printed agenda. The gavel had a small plaque on its handle, lauding her for ten seasons of distinguished service as chair of the League. Her re-election this year was again by acclamation; for the past eight years, she had run for the office unopposed. Most board members were parents of players and rotated off the board when their kids aged out of the program and moved up to juniors.

Kenmore Midget Baseball League had operated in Kenmore since shortly after World War II. In the 1960s, the organization had incorporated as a 501(c)(3) tax-exempt nonprofit organization. It formally incorporated for several reasons, but the principal motivation was to respond to the liability exposure members of the organization thought they might have from injuries players and spectators might suffer as a result of being hit by stray balls. An added benefit of this status was that individuals who made donations to the organization could deduct their value on their federal income tax forms.

League expenses consisted chiefly of equipment, field rentals, insurance, paying umpires, maintaining the fields, and painting the Clubhouse. In addition to an annual dinner dance fundraiser, income came from a modest $50/season fee assessed to players in the league (waived if a family could not afford it) and from tax-deductible contributions by team sponsors whose logos adorned the uniforms, ads sold for the program book, and signs put up on the electric scoreboard.

Sarah had been particularly proud of the scoreboard, for which she had found funding by requesting an earmark from a friendly state legislator who himself had played Midgets in Kenmore back in the 1970s.

Substantial additional income came from the brisk business generated by the field's concession stand, which had been operated by a local restaurant that was served by Sarah's food distribution business. That relationship was good for the equivalent of two team sponsorships each season. The agreement between the League and the restaurant was that 15% of proceeds would go directly to the League, and as an added bonus, the players playing in the game would receive a free hot dog and lemonade after the final out.

Volunteer parents staffed the concession stand each game, and this was the major activity in which parents engaged that contributed to the League's operations. The concession stand typically had a steady stream of customers whenever there were games. Many of the customers visited the stand without having any connection to the games, attracted to the reasonable prices for slushies, soft pretzels, roasted peanuts, grilled hot dogs, hamburgers, ice cream novelties, and popcorn. It was not unusual for the cash receipts at the end of an evening doubleheader to exceed $700. After each evening, when the concession doors were shuttered, Sarah would personally collect the cash from the register, count it, place it in a cash bag, and make a night deposit at the Kenmore Community Bank, another team sponsor.

Sarah was generally acknowledged as the glue that held all of the pieces together. Those close to the program's operations knew that she was not only the glue, but for the most part, was the pieces, as well. It was common knowledge that Sarah was indispensible to having a successful season. Almost single-handedly, she recruited coaches, arranged the schedule, hired the field maintenance crew (for the past two years now, comprised exclusively of her twin sons, who had once been stars for Kenmore's Allstars), ordered bats and balls, recruited sponsors, and made sure the uniforms were ordered.

She attended to every detail, including proofreading the designs of the uniforms to make sure the names of the sponsors were spelled correctly. The first year she had chaired the League, she had delegated that task, and was embarrassed to find that the Kenmore Indians sported jerseys that season sponsored by "Katy's Jewlers." Katie, the store owner, had expressed her disapproval, but had been mollified by being offered a free ad in the next year's program booklet. Sarah never delegated that task again, nor most others.

During the summer, Sarah was a professional volunteer, devoting much of her day to the League while her husband ran the family business. Each season, those who served on the board could count on Sarah to be a busy worker bee, making sure every task was completed. On the wall of the Clubhouse, in addition to team pictures of players and coaches, was tangible evidence of recognition of her efforts, of which she was justly proud. Among them was a copy of a proclamation of Kenmore Borough Council commending Sarah for her achievements, alongside a resolution passed by the State House recognizing her ten years of leadership as chair of the board.

Sitting in the stands watching the games on a warm summer evening was heaven to Sarah, basking in not only the sun, but the glow of knowing that this was a masterpiece she had created. Each year, she had added to this masterpiece until the facility and program were the envy of not only nearby communities, but of those around the state who visited, seeking advice on how to emulate the success of the Kenmore program. This year, she had arranged for the construction of pro-style dugouts, complete with a water fountain, courtesy of a cousin who ran a construction company. He had given her a good price and had completed the work well before the deadline. Among the accoutrements added in recent years were an electric scoreboard, a clubhouse (where this board meeting was being held) that housed the concession stand, and net-enclosed batting cages.

Although she solicited ideas for these improvements at board meetings, she generally decided on her own which new feature she would add. This was a closely guarded secret. Universally, there was admiration among the board for how she found ways to make the program better each year. A few board members might grumble about what they perceived as heavy-handed tactics, but no one disputed that the results she achieved were well worth the occasional ruffled feathers. Most respected the fact that Sarah did her homework before engaging in a project on behalf of the League, and she was not perceived at all to be a loose cannon risk taker. Admittedly, she was aggressive in building the League, and she acknowledged that there was some validity to the saying "you can't steal second base with one foot on first."

It was a relief for virtually every board member when they got a notice in their e-mail in January that a board meeting was to be scheduled at the Clubhouse located on the grounds of the Kenmore Midget Field. This served as verification that Sarah was again willing to not only serve as board chair, but likely would make all of the arrangements for the coming season. There was anticipation about what new, creative physical improvements would be made to the fields (or, as sometimes occurred, had already been made in the fall before the construction season came to a halt and before the field was ready for seeding and painting).

Sarah, on the other hand, lived for Midget Baseball, even now that her kids were grown. She was in charge and the League was hers to run without much interference from anyone. In previous years, when she first began taking a leadership role, she had delegated many of the tasks to other parents. But she found that it was rare that anyone else could produce the results required to assure that the product each summer was up to the high quality standards that she demanded and that the kids deserved.

Eventually, parents learned to let Sarah do everything herself and stay out of her way. They knew that Sarah's commitment would solve any problem that might come up, and it certainly saved them a lot of aggravation to let her do all of this work behind the scenes, which she apparently reveled in doing. On one level, they felt that they were exploiting her, but if she was willing to do all of this work, what was the harm? It wasn't like they were capitalizing on this by sitting at home eating bon bons. Most parents of players were busy with work, and in the evenings, they did chores, shopping, and helped their kids with their homework. If they were able to squeeze out an hour or two to relax with a shared TV program with their spouse or perhaps one night each week for a movie, they considered themselves lucky.

Being the parents of eleven-year-olds was so much different than it had been for their own parents. Midget League was not the only activity that required their attention. There were music lessons, religious school classes, and any other number of organized activities that required chauffeuring their kids and often waiting until the activity was completed to drive them home.

Almost to a parent, watching their son or daughter play in the Kenmore Midget League was something they looked forward to well before their child reached the eligible age to compete. Because everything about the program was first class, parents from outside Kenmore clamored for the opportunity for their kids to play their Midget baseball in that community. At first, the board had resisted opening up the program to outsiders in nearby communities, but eventually, it embraced doing so. More playing fields were added in Kenmore Park to accommodate the additional demand for teams.

At its peak the previous season, 10 teams of 14 players each were competing in the Kenmore Midget League. It was not unusual for the stands to have crowds exceeding 100 watching the games. Many graduates of the program went on to play high school and college baseball. Although no one had as yet reached the Big Leagues, two former players were playing AA minor league ball and were in a position to be called up to the Bigs in September.

After so many years of doing this work, Sarah could produce results effortlessly compared to having parents do their share and make a mess that she would have the task of cleaning up. Sarah knew which businesses in the community to squeeze for sponsorships, how to avoid scheduling games on religious holidays, which kids needed to be on separate teams, and how to placate the demands of "Little League Dads" who demanded that their teams consist of the best players. Dealing with some of these parents was the toughest part of Sarah's job, and she often had to serve as the sole arbiter when her coaches were unable to deal with the abuse they had to take for not starting a particular player. Or for taking that player out of a game "prematurely" to let a less talented player meet the League's requirement that each player on the team plays at least two innings in the field.

Sarah had even dealt with one mom who had heaped a constant tirade of abuse on the home plate umpire. Sarah had calmly informed that mom out of earshot of curious onlookers that her behavior was unacceptable and a violation of League rules—and that if she continued her behavior, she and her son would not only be banned from participating in any further competition, but that her husband would somehow find out who she was spending time with every Wednesday morning. The mom had backed down without indicating which threat had intimidated her the most.

Sarah had boundless energy when it came to League business, although during the season, everything else was relegated to secondary importance. One of her brood, in high school, had grown up in Kenmore Midgets, and was a promising pitcher, scouted by several major league teams. Another was an All-American college wrestler who also played for State on its baseball team. Sarah knew that without the experience of playing Midget baseball, many of the kids in Kenmore would have turned to drugs or a life of crime, and they might very well have become permanently entangled within the criminal justice system.

She was proud of her accomplishments. Several years earlier, she had even been nominated to receive one of the daily "Point of Light" awards, created in response to a call by President George Herbert Walker Bush in his 1989 inaugural address and spearheaded by the Points of Light Institute.

Although she was not independently wealthy, Sarah and her husband ran a successful local food distribution business, and they were more prosperous than most parents with kids on the teams. When she found out that a kid with some talent lacked a glove or proper cleats, she often reached into her own pocket to provide them. She was delighted when one of these kids started calling her "Mom," and other players started doing this, as well, making her feel proud. In some sense, they were all like her children to her.

In December, Lenny's Family Restaurant, the restaurant that operated the concession stand, had been forced to close because of lease problems. The owner had decided to move the restaurant to Centertown, more than fifty miles away from Kenmore. This development meant that the League would not only have to find two new team sponsors, but also find another operator for the concession stand.

This new problem didn't faze Sarah at all, as she was a problem solver. Sarah judged that she could kill two birds with one stone and turn lemons into lemonade, perhaps literally in this case. If her board had no objection, she would propose to take over the concession stand management, and continue the terms of the previous agreement, running everything through her husband's food distribution business. The revenues she would receive would pay for sponsoring the two teams that the restaurant had sponsored, and more so. She also calculated that doing this would compensate her for some of the countless hours she put in during all of these years of service. And it would solve a big problem, as it could take a lot of effort to find someone else to provide for concessions on short notice.

It would also help stop the constant nagging of her husband, who continually was complaining that Sarah's devotion to the Midget League, including long hours, was having a harmful effect on the family business and their own relationship, as well. Her husband suggested that it was not fair that Sarah did all of this work without any compensation, while others benefited and did virtually nothing. With no kids in the program any more, her dedication and generosity were being taken advantage of, he persistently pointed out.

Considering how much work went into each successful season, most of it done by Sarah single-handedly, it should be a paid position, he contended.

After consulting with her husband, she wrote down more details of her concession business plan that would bring some income into the household to compensate her for all of the work she was doing, without having to propose to the League that it hire her to do this work in the future. Obviously, if she decided for any reason not to continue doing this work as a volunteer, it would be difficult, if not impossible, for the program to continue. She made a note in her Blackberry to add this item to the board agenda, thinking that it was appropriate for the board to consider what she planned to do to solve this last-minute problem.

"The next agenda item is replacing the partnership agreement we had with Lenny's Family Restaurant to manage the concession stand. I've talked this over with my husband, and we are willing to take it on with the same terms of 15% of the revenue going to the League. My business will sponsor the two teams, and we will use parent volunteers as before. Things can go on and we won't miss a beat.

"Does anyone object?"

Discussion Questions:

1. Was it a problem that the concession stand was operated by a restaurant that had its food distributed to it by the board chair of the League?

2. How different does this situation become if the board chair herself is operating the concession stand?

3. What is the board's responsibility to question this proposal, and what is an appropriate response?

4. What problems might arise when an organization has one major committed volunteer who does all of the work? What might happen to the organization if that person burns out or otherwise becomes unable or unwilling to perform those duties? What leverage does that person have to make sure the board acts as he/she desires?

5. How should anyone in a nonprofit organization with authority to hire workers do so? What are some of the problems with how Sarah handles this process?

6. Would the governance structure of this organization benefit by having committees?

7. Some individuals find the use of the term "midget" to be derogatory, even when used in the context of a youth baseball league. Discuss how you would handle a situation as the chair of the Kenmore Midget League if a board member offered a motion to change the name of the organization to the "Kenmore Youth Baseball League" and to forbid the use of team names that may have been used in this League for years that might be offensive to some people, such as "Indians," "Redskins," and "Braves."

Case 15
The Professor's Farewell

Dr. Stephen Richards locked the door behind him, tested it carefully, and made the short trek from his office in the Social Sciences Administration Building to a classroom in Harrison Hall, behind the Woodson Library. It was a trip he had made hundreds of times. More than likely, this would be the last such trip in his academic career.

It was Friday, the last day of summer term, and few students were on campus. He remembered back when he had first arrived here, the ink on his Ph.D. diploma hardly dry, never suspecting that he would possibly be teaching the same courses for the same department at the same institution for four decades.

In those four decades, he had physically changed along with the campus. His beard was now grey, and his bones creaked when he walked down the polished granite stairs to the department's bank of elevators. Perhaps he had put on "only" two extra pounds each year, but they added up. Now 73, his obesity was only one of his chronic health problems, exacerbated by age and lack of exercise.

In contrast, the University had aged more gracefully, expanding away from the town's main street in three directions, sprouting up buildings of modern glass and concrete that changed the character away from the ivy-covered brick walls that he had known when first arriving. The University had a voracious appetite, particularly in the 1970s and 1980s, consuming nearby parking lots, small businesses, student and other low-income ramshackle housing, a couple of factories, and even a hospital. The acquisition of land for expansion was accomplished with some of the same ruthlessness, although not on quite the scale, as the early settlers of America had shown expanding westward at the expense of the indigenous population.

When he first taught here, locking doors of his office behind him had been unnecessary. But times had changed, not only on urban university campuses, but on relatively isolated bucolic campuses such as Tidwell University, as well. Several weeks earlier, someone had broken into the department's offices and made off with seven computers. Just this summer term, there had been two sexual assaults reported on campus, an armed robbery, a carjacking, and several dorm room break-ins.

On this Friday morning, the air was pungent with the odor of burning leaves. Although fall term was still three weeks away, leaves were dropping on campus, creating piles for a multitude of grey squirrels to scamper through, chasing each other playfully. Students were playing touch football on the quad, adjacent to the classroom building. *Oh, to be 19 again*, he mused.

I'll miss football, he thought to himself, reveling again in the memory of Tidwell just missing out on being in the NCAA Division 1 title game the previous season. When it came to football, the Tidwell administration gave that program a virtual blank check, even when there was a hiring freeze and a temporary ban on using department money to pay academic conference attendance expenses.

Tidwell had done everything legally possible, and sometimes not so legally, to improve its chances for national prominence that accompanied success on the gridiron. "Student" athletes were recruited to play for the institution, some of whom were functionally illiterate. For the glory of Tidwell, some students were provided with not only room, board, and books, but also full-time tutors and special classes. That was the best that could be offered, once the NCAA put a stop to the gifts of cash, cars, and clothes to star recruits from sports-obsessed alumni.

Some professors at Tidwell had resigned several years earlier rather than yield to the substantial pressure from the administration to give certain football players a break on their grades so they could remain eligible to play. Eventually, the administration had wised up and sequestered most of the football squad in their own classes, with their own professors, away from the "real" students. Doing so was expensive, but it had been a great investment. Donations from proud alumni soared with the nearly undefeated season last year, enough to fund not only the costs of the football program but of Tidwell's entire lineup of NCAA Division 1 sports for both men and women.

Although perhaps only a third of the football team's entering freshmen ever graduated, none of them ever questioned whether they were being exploited. On the contrary, most would have said their five years at Tidwell were the best of their lives, even if most were relegated to working in dead-end jobs rather than becoming millionaires as high draft choices on an NFL team, as many had expected to be when they accepted a scholarship offer to play for the legendary coach of Tidwell, Buckets Henry. It had been rumored for years that Coach Henry's salary was more than ten times that of the President of Tidwell, confirmed when the federal government required the top salaries of tax-exempt nonprofit organizations to be disclosed on the organization's 990 federal tax return. The line-item on the return, of course, did not include the income Henry received from his radio show, endorsements, and royalties on products.

The consensus was that since the Tidwell president had never personally led a Tidwell team to an undefeated national championship 13-0 season and a major bowl bid worth almost $15 million, the salary shelled out to Henry was worth every penny. Although this money had to be shared with other schools in the conference, the spike in sales of official clothing and souvenirs with the school's logo as a consequence of success on the gridiron more than compensated for this.

Twice in its history, the Tidwell board of directors had been forced to make a choice between keeping either the school's president or the football coach. It had not been one of the tougher decisions it had had to make.

Other than a year off almost 20 years ago for a well-deserved sabbatical leave, Dr. Richards had not missed teaching fall term in his 40 years with the University. This would be something he would miss the most. There was something magical about fall term. He would sometimes sit outside on a bench in the quad in early September, adjacent to one of the residence halls, and watch parents drop off their sons and daughters. Many of these children, now young adults, would be having their initial experience of being on their own, away from home for any extended period of time.

If it had been his choice, Dr. Richards would have continued to teach until he died or was unable to stand up in front of a classroom. And with the amazing state-of-the-art technology to which he had access, even the inability to stand up in a classroom would not have deterred him from physically being able to teach classes. The University had an active online master of public administration (MPA) program, and several years earlier, Dr. Richards had experimented by teaching one of the classes. It simply wasn't his cup of tea, he remembered. He could not look into the eyes of his students and see whether what he was saying was sinking in. Overall, he found that teaching online required much more work on his part. He did appreciate that the online environment encouraged his students to think about a response to a question. In a classroom, his students appeared to be in a competition to raise their hands first and be recognized (at least those who deigned to participate, which seemed to be declining with every passing year). Online, the playing field was leveled.

On the other hand, he could barely keep up with the rigors of online teaching. He did not have a good experience; the department had been forced to bring in a Ph.D. student to take over his class after the fourth week after students complained that he was two weeks behind in responding to classroom posts.

A realist, he recognized that the University would likely try to exploit the advantages of online education, as it could charge students full price for courses without all of the high overhead of having support facilities. It was indeed a lucrative enterprise. But he remained skeptical that students really learned anything of value. His department had lately been advertising for online adjuncts, recognizing that it could pay salaries that might be a third of what it would have to pay for recruited assistant professors, and it would avoid having to pay any benefits, as well. The jury was still out, in his mind, over whether students were learning anything by typing into a keyboard, perhaps in the middle of the night with loud rock music in the background and the air filled with marijuana fumes.

But who's to say they are learning anything of value in conventional classes, he mused. *Things have changed so much in 40 years.*

It was not really his choice to retire. He really wasn't sure why the department's leadership found him to be expendable after 40 years. Being a tenured faculty member, he technically couldn't be fired. In his younger days, he had considered the tenure process simply another strategy colleges and universities had adopted to institutionalize mediocrity.

No one in the administration had ever directly asked for his resignation; rather, it was a series of explicit and implicit messages, some subtle, some not so. Perhaps the first sign of his falling out of favor was his appointment to the Parking Appeals Committee. His applications to attend various academic conferences, once approved routinely, were now denied. He became more suspicious after he judged that his student advisor caseload had inexplicably doubled. He noticed that not only the administrators, but even faculty members whom he had mentored, were beginning to avoid him. Last year, he had received an e-mail notice that his office in the department's headquarters would need to be vacated to make room for a new research and teaching institute. He was able to harness what little political power he still had to reverse that decision of the academic dean, with whom his relationship had frayed since his failed attempt to thwart the University from accepting a sizeable donation from a convicted felon.

One obvious message came from his deteriorating course assignments. Lately, he was assigned to teach courses that were typically assigned to junior faculty, and at times of the day that were not particularly pleasant, such as this current class assignment at 8 a.m. on a Friday. Eventually, he was not assigned to teach much at all. Although this freed him to pursue more opportunities for his research, he knew that his *raison d'être* was teaching. Most of his research, he knew, would never be communicated to those who could use it to make the world better in any way. Rather, it would be published in academic journals that hardly anyone, even his colleagues, would even open, if only to see whose articles got published. When he had an article published in one of these journals, he could count on kudos being offered by his friends in the department and in his field. But he was well aware that hardly anyone actually read the articles, not that it would have changed any behavior in the world if anyone had read them.

At first, he fought against the pressure to retire. Last year, with resignation, he recognized that it was an uphill battle to continue to resist, and that the joy of teaching was dampened by the frustrations of dealing with an administration that he felt was openly hostile to serving the educational needs of students, making their own needs paramount. And the students seemed more interested in partying than learning.

Students today expected getting an "A" simply for showing up, he lamented. The grade inflation in recent years induced this attitude to some extent. And no wonder; professors were often judged by their student evaluations, and students who expected to get good grades gave their professors good evaluations. Students had the process of taking the easy way out down to a science; they shared intelligence on Web site databases to find out which professors were "easy." When he was a student himself, Richards had been more interested in determining which professors were good teachers. The good grades came through hard work. Getting an "A" was an achievement back then. Even then, flunking out was a real fear, even for students who had done well in high school.

Maybe it really is time for me to retire, he thought, entering the classroom. *I remember when the business of the University was run by educators whose sole concern was educating its students. Today, if there is an interest in preserving educational standards, it seems more that this is to preserve the value of the University's "brand name" rather than prepare our students to respond to global challenges. No wonder football has become such a high priority.*

Harrison Hall was a completely renovated and retrofitted building of classrooms, wired for the 21st century. Most of the funds for the renovation had been donated by William Jayson Harrison, whose net worth had been estimated at $400 million at the time of his conviction for insider trading violations. He had served his sentence in the federal penitentiary at Allenwood, often considered one of the "country clubs" for federal white collar criminals. There had been serious opposition from some board members and faculty about accepting the $30 million gift from Harrison to fund the classrooms, particularly since it was predicated on the requirement that the Hall bear the donor's name.

Richards himself, as a member of the Faculty Senate at the time, had argued against accepting the donation. He had pointed out that just as for-profit companies pay for the naming rights of stadiums, there is a tangible value to the donor for doing so. So, at a minimum, if the University wanted to prostitute itself (the very phrase he used) by selling its good name to benefit a convicted felon, the University should consider naming the building after Harrison as a fee for service, and should not issue Harrison a substantiation letter acknowledging that the $30 million was a gratuitous donation and thus eligible for a tax exemption.

As expected, the motion was made to endorse acceptance of the gift and it carried by a large majority. The school needed the money. Although tainted, a dollar was a dollar. From that day on, he had noticed his relationship with his department leadership, most of them 20 years his junior, had begun to fray.

He entered the classroom at exactly 8 a.m. He saw again that most of his class of 16, mostly upperclassmen in his Non-profit Management Seminar class, had not yet arrived. Most needed three elective credits that could be squeezed into their schedules on Fridays to avoid delaying their graduations, and they were understandably not particularly interested in the topic of the class.

Some, he suspected, had simply blown off the final class. Several years earlier, he had announced that being late to his classes was rude and disruptive, and that the door of his classroom would be locked from the inside when the clock's second hand hit twelve, the time the class was to start. That policy lasted exactly one week; four students who had been late the following week had jointly complained to the academic dean, and Richards was curtly informed that he should be a bit more accommodating to "customers."

The school had been on a Total Quality Management kick at that time. In successive years, it had gone through other business fads, including Management by Objectives, Future Search, and Business Process Reengineering. In virtually every case, the "reform" was accompanied by evaluations, surveys, tons of forms to fill out, and, as he had predicted, had resulted in little if any improvement in the efficiency or effectiveness of the University's programs and activities.

What he thought was the last straw, convincing him to consider his retirement, was a budget department policy that courses would be cancelled if they were not self-supporting. This meant that Richards' favorite Ph.D. seminar electives would not be held as scheduled, as it was unlikely that the population of Ph.D. students in the small program would support enrollment at the required minimum.

He had tried to organize a protest. If the institution would only offer courses that broke even or made a profit, how could they justify seeking donations? The response from his colleagues was lukewarm at best. No one wanted to rock the boat anymore, certainly not like almost everyone had seemed willing to do in the turbulent sixties when he had arrived on campus. He remembered an anti-war rally in progress on the quad when he had arrived for his interview. Students had briefly occupied the president's office, demanding an end to the ROTC program on the campus.

In the last ten years, the largest campus protest he remembered was one organized by the student newspaper when the board had approved a tuition hike of 10%.

He took his usual place behind a small lectern and looked over his class, its ranks depleted even more than its typical 75% attendance rate. When he had been an undergraduate, he had attended classes wearing a tie and jacket. Today, anything more than shorts and a T-shirt would be considered formalwear. The young women pretended to be oblivious to the effect their low-cut halter tops were having on their male colleagues, but likely were well aware. He, himself, pretended not to notice.

Students from all social classes sported spiked haircuts. Pink dyed hair. Nose rings. Fingernails looking more like talons with designs on them. And tattoos!

Students came to class with laptops, iPods, Blackberries, and other electronic gadgets that had been out of a science fiction comic book at the time he had been an undergraduate and now were *de rigueur* for almost everyone. All he had taken to class as a student was a book, a notebook to take notes, a pencil, and an empty, open mind, which he expected the professor to fill with wisdom. Today's student demanded two hours of entertainment and an opportunity to chat.

Professor Richards looked up, smiled as warmly as he could muster, and began the class.

"Good morning, everyone. This is the last class of summer term, and I hope you've enjoyed it as much as I have. I'd like to begin by going back to basics and discussing what makes an organization a nonprofit, what makes it a charity, and what is the difference between these two, and how nonprofit organizations differ from other organizations in government and the business sector."

His eyes met Roger, his best student, perhaps the only one who took the class seriously, who studied, and who he thought might have actually paid attention to his lectures. "Roger, let's begin with you. Why is Tidwell University considered a nonprofit, charitable institution?"

"Well, none of the excess revenue over expenses inures to the benefit of the trustees, and Tidwell offers scholarships to the needy."

"That's a good start. Now, let's assume that you are paying the full cost of your education, and something happens, so your parents no longer can pay your tuition. Should we assume that Tidwell will give you a discount of some kind, or treat you like any other for-profit business? What I mean is, will you be given a break based on your ability to pay, or will you be thrown out on your posterior, and escorted from the classroom if you expect Tidwell to act like a charity?"

"Thrown out on your ass, obviously," came a response from a possibly anorexic young woman with a nose ring and black lipstick, sitting in the back row.

"Now, look around this campus. It is about five times as large as it was when I first started working here 40 years ago. The annual budget of Tidwell University is perhaps $1 billion annually, in round numbers. The income Tidwell receives from its $12 billion endowment is more than that, because it has hired staff who invest its money in all sorts of business enterprises and securities. One could argue that the main business of the Tidwell Corporation is to generate wealth from its investments, and that education is simply a side business. So, if you accept that, why does Tidwell deserve to be tax-exempt?"

"Don't foundations have to distribute 5% of their assets annually?"

"No, this federal requirement doesn't apply to educational institutions, and even if it did, the 5% rule includes reasonable administrative expenses.

"Now, how many of you think Tidwell pays any property taxes? If Tidwell pays some of its endowment fund managers seven-figure incomes—certainly more than our university president earns—you might argue that it values this side of the 'business' more than education. So, how can it justify receiving a property tax exemption that by any estimate has a value more than the amount of scholarships Tidwell provides to needy students? Remember, we have already agreed that if you can't pay your tuition, you are barred from attending classes and are forcibly ejected from the campus, using our taxpayer-subsidized campus security force if necessary."

He didn't wait for any answers.

"And it is not like students know what they are getting into when they start here freshman year. Tuition was just $5,000 when I started teaching here; each year it increased by about twice the CPI. What other business can get away with offering a product to its customers without knowing in advance what the price is going to be, and having that product virtually worthless unless you pay up in full and graduate?

"What is the value of a four-year university education at Tidwell University if you take being awarded a diploma out of the calculation? Put another way, how much would you be willing to pay for it? And let's assume you could agree to have a four-year degree from Tidwell with the proviso that at the end of the four years, you would have your diploma, but everything you learned would be wiped clean from your memory? That is, you have the legitimate credential but not the learning, skills, or knowledge?"

Unlike in other class sessions, he saw evidence that his students were beginning to respond to his questions. At least they appeared to be shifting uncomfortably in their seats.

"Without having to go to school, take tests?"
"Without the partying and Bowl Games?"
"I would probably pay more for that than what the current tuition is!"

"Now, what if I told you a little secret about how Tidwell is run. This year, Tidwell's budget office sent a memo to all of the academic deans informing them of a new policy stating that each class we offer, with limited exceptions, needs to generate at least as much in revenue as its expenses. In other words, if a class has enrollment that is too low to generate a break-even point for the course, it will be cancelled. This, of course, is why this course was scheduled originally for spring term and is being offered in the summer—in addition to the fact that Tidwell pays professors less for teaching summer courses than for fall or spring courses. What are some of the unintended consequences of this?"

"Well, for one thing, students who need courses to graduate might not find the course offerings they need."

"How about, how do you justify asking alumni to donate—with the implication that their donations are subsidizing the education of students, when by definition, there is no longer a need for subsidization?"

"Is this why my class in strategic planning last term was taught by an adjunct faculty member?"

"Actually like, you know, one of my classes was taught by a master's graduate student. I bet he was barely paid at all. There were 30 students in the class, and we each were paying $600 per credit hour, or $1,800 for the class. I would expect that would generate some net income. Let's see, $1,800 times 30…."

"But you are forgetting that for every class like those, there are full professors earning six figures who might only be teaching a class or two each term, and who are instead getting paid out of your tuition money to do research. Research is an important part of teaching institutions such as Tidwell University. And there are costs, such as when the University pays the equivalent of hundreds of thousands of dollars to me to do research rather than teach, I send this research to an academic journal, which then publishes it—and charges the University to buy a subscription to that publication, and charges again for the right to make copies.

"Believe it or not, I get a notice from the journal telling me when my article appears that I have the right to purchase copies of my article. Once in a while, the journal offers me a small discount!"

"Are you making this up?"

Something about the story he was telling about research triggered a deluge of more stories, which he began nonstop. He could hardly focus on the class in front of him. Forty years of frustrations came out like a flood, induced by the ambivalence of emotions he felt upon reflecting that this was likely to be his final class. He couldn't help himself. For the next 90 minutes, Dr. Richards launched a monologue and shared with his class why he thought the education system was a failure, and why Tidwell University was in need of reform if it wanted to break the culture.

Why are professors usually such bad teachers? Because getting one's Ph.D. doesn't require any training on how to teach. I am certified to teach Ph.D. students, but I can't teach seventh grade in the Tidwell school district, because I don't have the certification required to do so...

When I first started here, there was virtually no crime. Ten years ago, the University saw the need to construct a building to house the expanded security department, which monitored the campus inside and out using a sophisticated video camera system. The institution now had an entire police force that was as large, and as well-trained, as that of the town of Tidwell itself. Four patrol cars are in the fleet. Each year, the security department puts in a request to purchase several AR-15 automatic assault rifles—the civilian version of the M-16—although the administration routinely denies funding for these—but it is only a matter of time before this request gets approved, now that college campuses have been victimized by mass shootings.

Did you know that you have the right to see reports of crimes on the Tidwell campus? The Congress enacted the Student Right-To-Know and Campus Security Act of 1990. *The law was further amended in 1998 to require most institutions of higher learning, including Tidwell, to keep a public crime log, and to impose sanctions against institutions that fail to accurately disclose crime on campus. This is one more example of how government regulates nonprofit organizations differently from business organizations. Before the federal mandate, Tidwell was quite protective about keeping its crime incidents to itself, so as not to blemish the institution's reputation. I remember how many eyes were opened when the first report of crime on campus was made public, and the internal debate that had preceded publication of the report on how to sanitize it as much as possible.*

He railed against the tenure system, which he suggested protects the mediocre. He criticized the disconnect between research and practice. He pointed out his view that tuition was higher because senior faculty members were being paid six-figure salaries for having a minimal teaching load, and the school was top-heavy with assistant deans each receiving high salaries and lucrative benefits who did the work previously performed by deans.

No subject about his experience at Tidwell was taboo.

...which raises another, related issue. Probably scores of faculty members have been involved in dealing with cover-ups involving alleged cases of sexual harassment at Tidwell, which in decades past had typically resulted in the victim quietly being forced to leave the University and little or no sanctions imposed on the perpetrator. Federal laws have been enacted to apply protections against sexual harassment on all workplaces, such as Title VII of the Civil Rights Act of 1964, *and on educational institutions receiving federal subsidies, such as Title IX of the* Education Act Amendments of 1972. *These laws give students legal ammunition to fight professors who thought of their students as potential members of their own private harem. This is another example of government regulation directed at nonprofits...*

He noticed several students peering down at their watches. It was 9:50, time for the class to be dismissed. Dr. Richards had just been getting warmed up. There was so much more to tell these poor souls who were trapped by the system.

"As some of you know, this is my last class before I retire. I have enjoyed teaching, and I hope that I have made a positive impact on the lives of my students. I didn't become a millionaire teaching. I did accomplish some things, and I have enjoyed it. So, I can only say 'farewell' and hope you learned something useful here, and will put to good use what you learned in this nonprofit management seminar. If you haven't provided it yet, please don't forget to turn in your final paper to me now or e-mail it to me by close of business today. Class dismissed."

The students gave him a standing ovation, as was customary at the conclusion of the last class of a course. He waited in the room until every student had left. Then he laid his head down on the desk, tears streaming down his face.

Two students left the classroom together, their arms draped around each other's backs. One male with spiked bleached hair and one female. Both were wearing earrings. His hand was buried in the back pocket of her jeans.

"Bit of a pompous, self centered jerk, don't you think?"

"I've had worse. At least he didn't give us a final exam. Gotta say, his two-hour rant for the entire last class was a bit over the top. How did you stand it?"

"I spent most of it playing Free Cell on my iPhone, and then I got bored, so I spent the rest of the time writing rude messages on my friends' Facebook walls. I know it's only 10, but let's go back to my dorm room and get wasted."

Roger, the professor's best student, went to the library to return some books. After he had done so, he sat in a corral and checked to see if anyone had posted any responses to his blog, which he had written and posted during Richards' class. Roger had dutifully chronicled the professor's entire rant in detail. *Should definitely get some comments on this one,* he anticipated. He was disappointed to find no responses yet, but the day was young. And, he was delighted by an @reply on Twitter, responding to his tweet about his new blog post. It read: *im a reporter for the Wash Post. Luvd yr blog today. Doing an article on ed reform. Pls call me. 202-334-7300 steve reedman*

Discussion Questions:

1. Review the public crime reports submitted by your campus's security department. Is anything surprising to you? What might be some of the reasons colleges and universities resisted the regulation to make these reports public? What might have been some of the reasons why the Congress enacted it over their objections?

2. Should donors to charities that condition their donation on naming a building after them be entitled to a tax-deduction?

3. What are the pros and cons of a charity accepting a donation from a convicted felon?

4. Why should Tidwell University be exempt from local property taxes? How much community benefit should institutions be providing before they are deemed to be eligible for such an exemption?

5. What are some of the unique aspects of nonprofit universities that make them different from other charities?

6. What are some of the unique aspects of nonprofit universities that make them different from for-profit or government institutions of higher learning?

7. Professor Richards remembers the days when students expressed their advocacy by holding rallies on campus. Discuss how social media such as Facebook, MySpace, and Twitter have given students new tools to coordinate their efforts when they seek change. How has social media changed the educational culture? How might it change in the future as a result of these new tools?

Case 16

Doctoring the Résumé—Giving the Third Degree to the Director of Research at SCRC

Dr. Mary Parker, executive director of the State Children's Research Consortium (SCRC), was sitting in front of her computer screen when she made a shocking discovery. She was aimlessly surfing the Internet in her office between meetings, at this particular moment, seeing what new posts of interest were made on Facebook. She had another meeting in ten minutes, for which she had procrastinated preparing. No matter; she had confidence she could wing it adroitly.

This new development was certainly more important. If what she read on this one particular posting about her most valuable staff member was true, she would rather pack up her briefcase, go home, and hide under the covers for at least a week.

Normally, she would have felt a bit guilty about indulging herself in such an activity on work time. But yesterday, while she was spending a few minutes decompressing after a tense meeting on her organization's potential budget shortfall by clicking on some links her cousin Lisa had shared via e-mail, she had come across news of a study conducted by researchers from the University of Melbourne on Internet surfing in the workplace.

According to the study, a large majority, 70% of the workers who were the study's sample population of 300, engaged in Workplace Leisure Internet Browsing (WLIB). WLIB was defined by the author of the study as browsing the Web for information and reviews of products, reading online news sites, playing online games, keeping current with friends' activities on social networking sites, watching videos on YouTube, and similar non-work related activities. What was surprising about this study was that the researchers determined that workers who engaged in WLIB were, overall, more productive than those workers who didn't spend work time on the Internet, at least when WLIB was limited to not more than 20% of work time. The researchers theorized that Internet surfing and other personal use of the Internet during work time afforded an unobtrusive break that helped workers' brains regain their concentration for work tasks.

With a chuckle to herself, she remembered one staff member she had had to let go for spending almost all of his time doing personal business while at work. She imagined that had he read the article, perhaps he might have decided to spend a few hours each day actually doing the work he was being paid to perform, as doing this might have made him think he would be able to focus better doing his personal business—at least so long as his time doing actual work for SCRC didn't exceed 20 percent of the time in the office.

Dr. Parker often accessed the Internet for personal purposes during work hours, but usually for only a brief time. Certainly nowhere near the 20-percent threshold. She was a busy member of the staff, dealing with five full-time researchers and a cadre of ten administrative and other support staff, not including herself. She used to feel guilty stealing a few minutes of down time, reading the latest posts on the *American Idol* blog or looking for a bargain on a new smart phone at Amazon.com. Her guilt during these forays away from her official duties in her office was somewhat assuaged after having read about the study. Now, if she could only find something about a study with a similarly counterintuitive conclusion that those who eat at least one bar of chocolate each day were more successful in losing weight than those who didn't!

The Consortium's primary mission was to conduct research to improve the health outcomes of children. Although some of the studies the Consortium conducted required its researchers to collect their own data, the organization mostly analyzed existing data, such as that collected by the State's Health Care Cost Containment Council (HCCCC), a quasi-governmental organization that was a collaboration of the State Department of Health and the State Hospital Association, authorized by a statute enacted a decade earlier by the State Legislature. Many of the research studies conducted by SCRC were commissioned by the HCCCC. Funding for these studies came mostly from the HCCCC and from grants from some of the largest and most prestigious national foundations concerned about the health of children.

SCRC was incorporated as a federal, tax-exempt 501(c)(3) organization, with a board consisting of a balanced mix of health researchers, hospital administrators, elected officials, community advocates, academics, and representatives of think tanks in the state. Doing so provided many advantages compared to creating the organization simply as a research arm of the Department of Health. Generally, the board stayed out of Mary's way, and she had developed a close relationship with her funders.

Although Dr. Parker suspected others on her staff wasted working time playing computer games, arranging personal trips, or reading movie reviews, she wouldn't have considered cracking down on this practice. She never monitored how her staff used their time, provided they accomplished what needed to be done. She trusted their judgment in using their time. If they required an afternoon off to attend to some personal business, she routinely granted it, provided they did not have important deadlines that would be missed. She did not feel it was necessary to hold her staff hostage until 4:30 p.m. each work day.

Mary often enjoyed using the Google search engine to take a break from the pressures of running the largest research organization in the state devoted to children's health. Periodically, she would Google the names of her employees and their families and visit the social networking profiles of those who had one. She took pleasure in learning about her coworkers' personal lives. Many of the professional staff had joined the organization when she had four years ago, and everyone was collegial and friendly. It was not unusual for staff members to invite the entire SCRC staff to their life-cycle events. There were staff outings to sports events, picnics, and occasional dinners. It would have been natural for the staff to be segregated culturally along the lines of educational achievement. It was important to her to make sure that those who had their Ph.D.s treated those who didn't as equal, valued members of the team.

Dr. Parker would have been the first to admit that her role was mostly administrative and political. She had been a researcher once herself, but her current role was to assure that the SCRC had the resources it needed to fulfill its mission and keep all of its stakeholders happy. Perhaps her most important task for the organization was recruiting some of the best talent around to design and carry out the research that she knew would be used by state and local government, foundations, and practitioners in the field to improve the health outcomes of children, many of them disadvantaged. And, of course, doing what was necessary to retain these staff and keep them happy and motivated.

One of the best decisions she had made, she had thought, was hiring Harry Hauser as the Director of Research. Dr. Hauser was amazing, and his commitment to the mission of the Consortium was unquestionable. He was responsible for the five-member research department, all of whom had Ph.D.s. No study had ever been conducted by the organization since his arrival that did not have his creative signature visible somewhere on it, increasing its chances to avoid any threats to internal and external validity. In some cases, his research designs were a work of art, and several state laws were directly attributable to the data he collected and analyzed.

She was in the habit of cleansing her browser's history after each WLIB session, so as not to be embarrassed if anyone was snooping on her computer. This time, she bookmarked the Facebook page she had just accessed. She also printed out the page, as well, and placed it in a secured personnel file cabinet. More than likely, this particular post would be deleted as soon as Harry saw it.

Now, as she stared at the Facebook page on her computer screen for perhaps the tenth time, she could hardly believe what she was seeing, and wondered whether it might simply be a mistake. After all, there was no system in place that verified the accuracy or reliability of what one read on the Internet. Most of it was unfiltered, giving any single individual with a modem, some free open source software, and a Web hosting account the power to publish anything at any time. Social networking sites such as Facebook eliminated the need for even some of these minimal requirements.

What had shocked her was a comment on Harry Hauser's Facebook wall. Harry was one of Dr. Parker's 89 Facebook "friends." All of what she read on Harry's Facebook wall today was benign, other than one glaringly disturbing post. It was by all appearances from an Arkansas woman, a former colleague of Dr. Hauser's from a previous research job. She had been simply catching up with him, one of several new friends he had added this week. The post was written in a friendly manner and didn't appear to be malevolent in any way. But what Dr. Parker distilled from the posting was that Dr. Hauser had been dismissed from a similar research position in Arkansas four years earlier for exaggerating his academic credentials.

Dr. Hauser was, according to the post, Mr. Hauser. It raised the strong possibility that he had never received a Ph.D., although at the time of his dismissal from the Arkansas position, he was apparently quite proficient, if not gifted, in conducting research.

Dr. Parker had remembered building her staff and making a phone call to the executive director of that Arkansas organization that was Hauser's previous employer. Dr. Hauser's, or rather Mr. Hauser's, boss had praised his work, but had mentioned, somewhat cryptically, that he had left for personal reasons, and he had parted company on good terms. If the post was true, it wouldn't have been improbable that the terms of separation with that employer had been that his supervisor would have agreed not to disclose anything substantive about the reasons why Hauser had left the organization.

Dr. Parker considered how to deal with this upsetting situation. If the Facebook post was accurate, Dr. Hauser had won the keen competition for his well-paid position based on false pretenses. He certainly demonstrated that he had the expertise and qualifications to continue in the position if she decided to simply ignore what she had found. On the other hand, ignoring this information, she judged, made her complicit to his alleged fraud, and it wasn't fair to keep someone on her staff who was dishonest, even if this meant losing a valued employee.

She considered seeking advice from a friend (a real friend, not a Facebook friend), or sharing what she learned with the current board chair, an older philanthropist who usually told her to do whatever she needed to do, provided it was ethical and consistent with the organization's mission. However, she decided that once she shared this information with anyone, it would be only a matter of time before others learned of this. And even if she decided to keep it to herself, others could learn about Hauser's fraudulent credentials in the same manner as she had.

On one hand, she knew that silence was complicity, and it just wasn't right to ignore this information. And on the other hand, she knew that Hauser's research, using the substantial resources provided by the Consortium with funding from both public funds and prestigious foundations, was so valuable that thousands of lives of children at risk could very well be improved if she simply kept mum about what she had discovered.

This was shaping up to be a classic ethical dilemma.

Dr. Parker's ethics training in graduate school had prepared her to deal with ethical dilemmas, or so she thought. She recalled the two primary approaches to ethics—*teleological,* based primarily on the outcomes of a decision, and *deontological,* based primarily on principles. In this case, a teleological approach militated for keeping her mouth shut as long as possible, knowing that the greater good would be served. And a deontological approach suggested her taking action on the principle that Hauser should be held accountable for his dishonesty—assuming the Internet post was accurate. And she truly hoped it wasn't.

She considered estimating the costs and benefits to each of the stakeholders of the organization, including herself, of various responses. She made an attempt to be a rational decision-maker, using her graduate degree nonprofit management training. The basic model she remembered was a seven-step process called RESPECT. In short, it called for:

- Recognizing the moral aspects of the dilemma,
- Enumerating the guiding principles,
- Specifying the stakeholders and their principles,
- Plotting the various options to resolve the problem, and evaluating these alternatives,
- Consulting with others, including the stakeholders, where appropriate, and
- Telling the stakeholders what your decision will be.

This model sounded reasonable in the crucible of a class, but in a real situation, she found it to be hopeless. There were too many variables, the issues were too complex, and the reaction of any single stakeholder to the news of Harry's deception, or rather alleged deception, in the calculation was unpredictable.

It was time for her next meeting, and she was so preoccupied with this new problem that she was unable to focus on the topic, which was whether to change the Consortium's health benefit plan and other fringe benefits to accommodate same-sex partners. Her distraction was noticed by other staff members around the table, but they plodded on until there was agreement to end the Consortium's current discrimination against gays and lesbians in committed relationships and propose this policy change for board approval.

When she returned to her office, she decided that her course of action would be to go with what her gut told her was the right thing to do, rather than weighing the costs and benefits through some calculation. Maybe the Facebook posting was a practical joke, she thought, thinking that this was unlikely. Almost every Ph.D. she knew who received a degree in the social sciences was more than willing to volunteer, unasked, the horror stories of his or her matriculation experience, the hazing, the senseless rewrites of dissertation chapters, and the months of delay until a dissertation chair set aside the time to read anything. Harry had never mentioned much about his doctoral experience at Princeton, which she found to be unusual. He had been reticent in response to her sharing her own story as an ABD student ("all but dissertation"), which had been the two worst years of her life.

Anxiety was mounting for her about how to deal with this, or whether to deal with it at all. The safest course was to simply sleep on it for at least a day. But she suspected that she would be unable to sleep soundly, knowing that this 800-pound gorilla in the room would make it difficult for her to have the interaction with Harry during working hours that she needed to do her job.

If only he wasn't such an important part of the success of this organization, she thought. The decision would be easy. But, she lamented, by all measures, Harry Hauser was a crackerjack researcher, regardless of whether he was Dr. Hauser or Mr. Hauser. His research designs were elegant. Although others performing research in the social sciences were content to distribute a survey to a sample population with a perfunctory Likert scale and simply publish the results, Harry found ingenious experimental designs that provided much more confidence that the answers to the research question posed were reliable and valid.

Harry had contempt for surveys, which he was unable to disguise even when doing so would have been appropriate. Surveys provided an opportunity for people to either lie, exaggerate, or self-delude themselves in order to please the researcher or be deceptive about personal issues. He was fond of illustrating this assertion by relaying the story of the Milgram experiments conducted in the 1960s. She remembered this as if it were yesterday, although it had in fact been several years ago.

Using newspaper ads and direct mail, Milgram recruited male individuals to participate in an experiment lasting an hour, for which they would be paid $4.50, paid whether or not the subjects completed the task. Subjects were told that they would be involved in an experiment that would test the effect of punishment inflicted by a teacher on learning, and would play the role of the teacher or learner. Unknown to the subjects, they always were picked to play the role of teacher, and a paid actor in cahoots with the experimenter was trained to play the role of learner. The learner, who made sure he informed the "teacher" that he had a heart condition, would pretend to receive a shock administered by teachers, and occasionally scream in mock pain and beg for mercy. The subjects were subjected to a 45-volt electric shock, as an example of the punishment the learner would receive with a wrong answer. They were then told to administer a shock to the learner when the learner gave a wrong answer to a question. Not knowing that the learner was not really a participant like themselves, they "administered" severe electric shocks when asked to by the experimenters. Most of the teachers were willing to administer electric shocks to the learners, who pretended to writhe in extreme pain and discomfort, and more than half (26 of the 40 subjects) administered "shocks" of 450 volts with either little or no encouragement from the experimenter before the experiment was halted.

Today, the methodology of this experiment is considered unethical. And it is. But if the methodology were carried out by traditional surveys, the result would be closer to the results obtained by Milgram when he asked his Yale senior psychology class what percentage of teachers they would predict would be willing to administer the severe shocks—which was less than 2%.

What point had Harry been making with this? He had continued with the punch line of the story.

> *Imagine the Milgram data had been collected relying on surveys administered to participants, as is the typical data collection tool for most social science research—*
>
> *Question #1: If you were asked by an authority figure to administer a 450-volt, potentially fatal shock to a heart patient, would you do so?*
>
> *Question 2: If "no," what would be the highest voltage you would administer?*

Using this philosophy, Harry's research often made the local news and occasionally made the national news, and certainly his research designs were legendary. The organization had exploited Harry's reputation for finding ingenious ways to answer sensitive questions by applying for a series of grants from the Hughsport Foundation. These grants not only funded all of Harry's salary, but also covered a good share of the general overhead of the organization. These grants not only had financial benefit, but there was a certain level of prestige that accrued whenever the Hughsport Foundation approved another grant.

Harry's contributions to the organization went beyond his research talents and his ability to attract outside funding from grantors. He was a model employee. Mary considered him to be a personal friend.

After the meeting on same-sex benefits, Mary returned to her office and tried to work. Instead, she began looking at movie reviews on the Web. Her thoughts returned to her dilemma, and she couldn't focus on the reviews.

She decided to confront Harry directly, to simply press his intercom button and ask that he come to her office. If anything, she might find some swift resolution. He could vehemently deny the truthfulness of the Facebook post, which would require her to investigate further. Or he might admit his subterfuge and beg to remain on staff. Or he might simply resign. Each of the three posed serious risks for the organization. This would likely be a distasteful confrontation, regardless of how sensitively she handled it, but she admitted to herself that as executive director, this was part of her job to do. Her instincts were to pose a simple question and to listen as much as possible.

She paged him to her office, and his head popped in.

"Sit down, Harry."

"Everything okay?"

"No. I just learned that you may not really have a Ph.D. from Princeton. If this is true, I haven't given much thought to what should be done about this, but I wanted to hear directly from you whether this was true or not."

She saw his face redden.

"It's true," he admitted. "I don't have a Ph.D. from Princeton. I was ABD at Princeton, but never got the chance to defend my dissertation. I kept running into roadblocks. The closer I thought I got, the farther away I seemed to be. And then my wife got pregnant, we had our first child, and you already know this, our kid had health problems. Eventually, he was diagnosed with autism. That has been one of my motivations for working with the Consortium, helping to identify treatment protocols to deal with problems such as what my son is experiencing. As a result of all of the stress of the Ph.D. program, needing to earn a living, and being a caregiver for my kid, I had to abandon Princeton when I was this close to finishing," he said, his fingers in the air indicating that he was really close.

"The truth is, I was as close to getting my Ph.D. from Princeton as one can get, and it certainly wasn't my fault that I didn't get through the last hoop they put in front of me. Obviously, my work here is good and respected nationwide, and the fact that I didn't get my Ph.D. diploma from Princeton didn't affect the quality of my research. My Ph.D. is really from Coolidger University. I could tell you more about this, but it is not something I am proud of. The short answer is that Coolidger is a diploma mill. It was the only way I was going to be Dr. Hauser.

"I lied on my application to work here. I admit that. I am sorry. If you want to fire me, I will understand. However, you might consider the option of disciplining me for lying on my job application in some way we can mutually agree, and keeping me on staff here. I need the job. I like working here. My research is first rate. No one has ever complained. Obviously, the mission of the Consortium is important to me, and I think everyone is served by letting me continue to do the job you hired me for, for which I am qualified."

"I appreciate your honesty," Mary shared. "I don't know how to respond, but there are issues here that I have to think through, such as who should be aware of this, and what authority I have to make the decision. So, give me the rest of the week to sort through this, and I'll meet with you to decide how we will address this."

"Again, I'm sorry. I always expected someone would find out eventually. Believe it or not, I am actually relieved that you now know about this." He got up and left her office.

Dr. Parker considered the option of simply keeping the information to herself and telling Harry to terminate his Facebook account, or at least remove the offending post and remove that former colleague as a Facebook friend. After all, it wasn't the same as if Dr. Hauser was claiming to be a medical doctor and performing surgery. Unlike in medicine, those without being formally trained in research can be quite capable of doing research. There is no requirement that researchers be licensed or even have any particular educational training. The proof was in the pudding that Dr. Hauser, or rather Mr. Hauser, knew what he was doing when it came to performing social science research, and his work was respected.

Clearly, he would not have been considered for the position with only a Master's degree, regardless of his abilities. The recruiting notice explicitly required an earned doctorate for applicants to be considered.

Epilogue: Five years later, Dr. Parker, still the executive director of the SCRC, comes across a news item about a research study, in which Dr. Harry Hauser is the senior project manager. It mentions that Dr. Hauser received his Ph.D. from Princeton University.

Discussion Questions:

1. What are some of the advantages the SCRC enjoyed by having incorporated as an independent nonprofit organization compared to being an office within the State's Department of Health?

2. What boundaries should there be between the personal and professional lives of staff members of a nonprofit organization? Should an executive director encourage or discourage staff to share time away from the office?

3. Should Hauser be fired simply because he misrepresented his credentials when he was hired, or are there other ways to discipline him while keeping him in the organization?

4. How might this development affect the credibility of the research he has already completed for the foundations and government agencies that commissioned his research?

5. Should Dr. Parker inform the funders of Dr. Hauser's past research that he lied about his credentials?

6. If Dr. Parker does fire him, does she have an obligation to tell funders who are expecting Hauser to be the senior project director for several major current grants?

7. If she does choose to fire him, what obligation does she have to disclose to future employees that he had misrepresented his credentials?

8. How much time is "permissible" for workers to do personal things such as surfing the Internet during work hours without being disciplined?

9. Was Dr. Parker's strategy for dealing with her initial confrontation with Hauser a good one? How else could she have approached this?

ORDER FORM

I would like to order the following:

Qty.	Item	Amount
_____	Nonprofit Management Casebook @ $16.95	_____
_____	The Nonprofit Handbook @ $29.95	_____
_____	The Pennsylvania Nonprofit Handbook @ $34.95	_____
_____	Fundraising Online @ $29.95	_____
_____	Introduction to the Nonprofit Sector @ $34.95	_____

Please send my order to:

Name _____

Organization _____

Address _____

City_____ State____ Zip_____

Telephone _____

Please send me more information about ❑social work publications and ❑nonprofit management publications available from White Hat Communications.

Sales tax: Please add 6% sales tax for books shipped to Pennsylvania addresses.

Shipping/handling:
❑Books sent to U.S. addresses: $8.00 first book/$1.50 each add'l book.
❑Books sent to Canada: $12.00 per book.
❑Books sent to addresses outside the U.S. and Canada: $15.00 per book.

Payment:
Check or money order enclosed for $_____
U.S. funds only.

Please charge my: ❑MC ❑Visa ❑AMEX ❑Discover
Card #: _____

Expiration Date _____

3-4 digit security code (back of card for VISA/MC/DISC; front of card for AMEX)_____

Name on card: _____

Billing address (if different from above): _____

_____

Signature: _____

Mail this form with payment to:
WHITE HAT COMMUNICATIONS, P.O. Box 5390, Dept. CS1
Harrisburg, PA 17110-0390
Questions? Call 717-238-3787.
Credit card orders: call 717-238-3787 or fax 717-238-2090
or order online at http://www.whitehatcommunications.com

More Nonprofit Management Books from White Hat Communications

An Introduction to the Nonprofit Sector: A Practical Approach for the 21st Century (Second Edition)
by Gary M. Grobman

An Introduction to the Nonprofit Sector: A Practical Approach for the 21st Century is an introductory text on the nonprofit sector and nonprofit organizations. It provides an overview of the history, theory, and scope of the nonprofit sector. It discusses issues facing nonprofits, such as legal and regulatory issues, ethics, quality, fiscal, and liability issues. It also provides practical guidelines for writing mission and vision statements, strategic planning, hiring, firing, lobbying, communicating, using the Internet, and other functions of nonprofit organizations. Each chapter includes a synopsis at the beginning, as well as discussion questions, activities, and bibliographic references at the end. An index is included. **Note:** This is the textbook version of *The Nonprofit Handbook: Everything You Need to Know to Start and Run Your Nonprofit Organization.*

345 pages•8½ x 11•ISBN 1-929109-19-9•2007•$34.95 plus shipping

---

Fundraising Online: Using the Internet to Raise *Serious* Money for Your Nonprofit Organization
by Gary M. Grobman and Gary B. Grant

Search engine marketing, blogs, personal fundraising pages, and podcasting are just a few of the strategies and techniques outlined in this handbook to assist fundraisers in harnessing the power of the Internet. This guide outlines a step-by-step approach to taking advantage of the e-philanthropy revolution, including a discussion of the pros and cons of soliciting funds on the web and an evaluation of creative business models. A chapter on developing a strategic online fundraising plan and a section on how to successfully engage in nonprofit e-commerce are also included.

In the sometimes wild kingdom of the Internet, there are pretenders to the throne, and then there are Gary Grobman and Gary Grant. Their new book, with its sweeping examination of all facets of online fundraising, trumps everything else on the market. Fundraising Online is a roaring success and should help you become one, too.

Jerry Cianciolo, Editor, *Contributions Magazine*

189 pages•8½ x 11•ISBN: 1-929109-18-0•2006•$29.95 plus shipping

The Nonprofit Handbook: Everything You Need to Know to Start and Run Your Nonprofit Organization (Fifth Edition)
by Gary M. Grobman

This 518-page, 36-chapter Handbook is based on *The Pennsylvania Nonprofit Handbook,* a book originally published in 1992 with the help of more than two-dozen nonprofit executives and attorneys and now in its 8th edition. Each easy-to-read chapter includes a synopsis, useful tips, and resources to obtain more information. Web addresses are included to obtain important government forms, instruction booklets, and informational publications. This essential reference tool includes:

- Information about current laws, court decisions, and regulations that apply to nonprofits—two full pages devoted to each state and the District of Columbia
- Practical advice on running a nonprofit, including chapters on grant-writing, communications, fundraising, quality management, insurance, lobbying, personnel, fiscal management, nonprofit ethics, and 27 other chapters
- Information on applying for federal and state tax-exempt status
- How to write effective grant applications

518 pages•8½ x 11•ISBN 1-929109-20-3•2008•$29.95 plus shipping

The Pennsylvania Nonprofit Handbook: EverythingYou Need to Know to Start and Run Your Nonprofit Organization (Eighth Edition)
by Gary M. Grobman

This is the Pennsylvania version of the above title. First published in 1992, this 399-page, 33-chapter *Handbook* includes a synopsis, useful tips, and resources to obtain more information. Web addresses are included to obtain important government forms, instruction booklets, and informational publications. This essential reference tool includes:

- Pennsylvania-specific Information about current laws, court decisions, and regulations that apply to nonprofit organizations
- Practical advice on running a nonprofit, including chapters on grant-writing, communications, fundraising, quality management, insurance, lobbying, personnel, fiscal management, nonprofit ethics, and 24 other chapters
- Information on applying for federal and Pennsylvania tax-exempt status
- How to write effective grant applications

399 pages•8½x11•ISBN 978-1-929109-22-7•2008•$34.95 plus shipping

ALSO PUBLISHED BY WHITE HAT COMMUNICATIONS:

BOOKS

An Introduction to the Nonprofit Sector:
A Practical Approach for the Twenty-First Century
by Gary M. Grobman

The Nonprofit Handbook
by Gary M. Grobman

Fundraising Online: Using the Internet to Raise Serious
Money for Your Nonprofit Organization
by Gary M. Grobman and Gary B. Grant

The Pennsylvania Nonprofit Handbook
by Gary M. Grobman

Days in the Lives of Social Workers
edited by Linda May Grobman

More Days in the Lives of Social Workers
edited by Linda May Grobman

Days in the Lives of Gerontological Social Workers
edited by Linda May Grobman and Dara Bergel Bourassa

The Field Placement Survival Guide
edited by Linda May Grobman

The Social Work Graduate School Applicant's Handbook
by Jesús Reyes

MAGAZINE

The New Social Worker—The Magazine for Social Work
Students and Recent Graduates

VISIT OUR WEB SITES

www.socialworker.com
www.socialworkjobbank.com
www.whitehatcommunications.com